NONI FLOWERS

Noni Flowers

40 Exquisite Knitted Flowers

6 Beautiful Projects

NORA J. BELLOWS

POTTER
CRAFT

NEW YORK

Copyright © 2012 by Nora J. Bellows

Published in the United States by Potter Craft,
an imprint of the Crown Publishing Group,
a division of Random House, Inc., New York.
www.crownpublishing.com
www.pottercraft.com

POTTER CRAFT and colophon is a registered trademark
of Random House, Inc.

Library of Congress Cataloging-in-Publication Data
Bellows, Nora J.
    Noni flowers : 40 exquisite knitted flowers / Nora J. Bellows. — 1st
ed.
        p. cm.
    Includes index.
    ISBN-13: 978-0-307-58671-1 (alk. paper)
    ISBN-10: 0-307-58671-5 (alk. paper)
    1. Knitting—Patterns. 2. Artificial flowers. I. Title.
    TT825.B385 2012
    746.43'2—dc23
                                                2011019991

Cover and interior design by Jenny Kraemer
Photography by R. A. Sullivan
Photographs on pages 12, 34, 158, and 176 by Kellie Nuss

Technical editing by Charlotte J. Quiggle

The author and publisher would like to thank the Craft Yarn
Council of America for providing the yarn weight standards
and accompanying icons used in this book. For more information,
please visit www.YarnStandards.com.

Printed in China
10 9 8 7 6 5 4 3 2 1

First Edition

FOR MY GRANDMOTHER, EMILY HAMMOND BELLOWS, 1903–2003,
THE GARDENER WHO WENT BEFORE ME.

AND FOR MY SON, SAMUEL "SOMA" HAMMOND AKKERMAN,
THE GARDENER WHO FOLLOWS ME.

"If you take a flower in your hand and really look at it, it's your world for the moment."

—Georgia O'Keeffe, *One Hundred Flowers*

SUNFLOWER – HELIANTHUS ANNUUS ⋮ ORIENTAL LILY – LILIUM ORIENTAL ⋮ CYCLAMEN – CYCLAMEN HEDERIFOLIUM

CHIONODOXA – CHIONODOXA FORBESII ⋮ DOGWOOD – CORNUS FLORIDA ⋮ DAHLIA – DAHLIA

TULIP – TULIPA HYBRIDA ⋮ PANSY – VIOLA TRICOLOR ⋮ CROCUS – CROCUS CHRYSANTHUS

Contents

Preface

This book is an homage to, and an exploration of, what I find in the woods I walk through and in the garden where I work in the morning. If I were a nineteenth-century woman, perhaps I would use a small pocket sketchbook and a pencil or watercolors to capture the flowers that inspire me. But my medium is silk, merino, mohair, lace-, and worsted-weight yarn. My instruments are knitting needles. With these tools, I've tried to re-create a little of the botanical beauty I see every day and share it with you.

I come from a long line of passionate gardeners. Family stories and photographs make me want to revisit their landscapes and to plant the things they planted. There are several cherished pictures of my great-grandfather, Alfred Hammond—or "Old Man," as he was affectionately called—with plants that seem to have grown beyond their normal limits under his care. A fading but finely grained photograph of Old Man shows him next to his "sun-towers," as one friend named the 18-foot-tall sunflowers he grew.

Old Man's brother, Henry, grew what became not a camellia garden, but a camellia forest. After a well-known horticulturalist told Uncle Henry the soil on his estate was not fit for camellias, declaring that he would never grow a single one, Uncle Henry proceeded to order truckloads of humus, peat moss, and other soil amendments. He had, at the time of his death, over two thousand camellias on his property, including some of the rarest in the world. They grew under a canopy of pines and were as big as trees themselves.

Emily Hammond Bellows, my grandmother, was similarly inclined toward a wild, wooded garden. She kept a journal of the flowers that bloomed each year around her house and in what numbers. She plotted the blossoms of hellebore and blackberry lily. She counted the blooms on her pink amaryllis, tallying the totals sometimes in pencil, sometimes in pen. While growing up, I didn't understand my grandmother's recordings, her version of the nineteenth-century woman's sketches and paintings. But at that time I didn't yet look forward to the tulips the way I do today. It's only now, after making and living with several gardens, that I've begun to appreciate more fully *her* garden and her devotion to it. I understand now why she loved the texture of foliage as much as the splendor of flowers, the complexity of the hosta lily's leaf, the lace of the fern and its primal fiddlehead, the pungency of the boxwood at the side door.

With every flower I have designed for this book, I have thought of my grandmother. Oh, how she would have *loved* these knitted blossoms.

Introduction

The task of the nineteenth-century gentle farmer-scientist was to explore the details of our world. Flowers were dissected, labeled, their jewel-like structures marveled at. These days, we take the microscope and all the detail it reveals somewhat for granted, and yet, a study of details is something of a rare thing. We look at flowers from a distance. We enjoy a profusion, we like great numbers of them in vases, we settle for a distant celebration of their beauty.

Here I bring forty select flowers close through the process of knitting them. I've sought to interpret a truth about each flower by using the architecture of actual flowers to suggest how the knitted versions must be formed. For example, a close inspection of the Oriental lily reveals a delicate, pale green spine that begins at the base of the petal, causing it to appear almost folded. It is this spine that is responsible for the petal's dimension. A field of pale green purl stitches, made distinct from the startling white of the rest of the petal's luminous cellulose through the technique of intarsia, mimics this aspect of the flower as well as possible using the seemingly strange medium of yarn.

I first started designing knitted flowers years ago to embellish the felted bags I created for Noni, my design company. I added a line of knitting patterns for my felted bags, flowers, and accessories in 2005, and Noni became known for modern bags and the flowers that embellished them. But this book has allowed me to take the knitted flower to a higher level of detail and realism than a single sheet pattern could possibly allow.

The flowers you find in these pages offer an abundance of choice. Their complex shapes can be realized not only with a set of standard knitting techniques, but with any sort of yarn you desire. Each flower can be a delicate embellishment or a true-to-size replica of its botanical counterpart simply by changing fiber type, yarn weight, and needle size. Every flower can be felted or left in its original knitted state. In many cases, I have photographed both the felted and unfelted versions side by side: The unfelted ones show every delicate stitch while the felted versions often appear more lifelike. And the projects I've included are simply the beginning of the many ways you can use these flower creations to decorate the spaces and objects around you.

HOW THE SAMPLES WERE MADE

The majority of the samples in this book were made using worsted- or light worsted–weight yarn worked on size 6 (4mm) needles. I recommend knitting densely. On size 6 needles: 20–22 stitches and 28–30 rows over 4" (10cm), 5–5½ stitches to 1" (2.5cm). For more delicate flowers, I used a lace- or fingering-weight yarn worked on size 1 (2.25mm) needles. For flowers I intended to felt, I generally used the same size needles; however, if you are concerned about shrinkage, you may use needles one or two sizes larger, so size 7 (4.5mm) or 8 (5mm) needles for the majority of the flowers, or size 3 (3.25mm) for the more delicate ones.

Because the flowers can be made on any size needle using any gauge yarn, *I did not include gauge or needle size information with the flower patterns.* Nor have I specified a particular gauge yarn. Instead, I've only listed the yarn colors necessary, leaving needle size and yarn choice up to you. Using the same set of instructions, the flowers in this collection can be lace-weight embellishments for infant sweaters, ballet slippers, and lingerie, or huge, dramatic centerpieces, depending on the needle and yarn selections you make.

I *have* indicated the specific yarn I used to make the samples pictured for those who would like to replicate my work. Small flowers will only require a few yards, one ball or skein of each color at the very most—this will usually make *many flowers,* whereas larger flowers will require more yarn; please purchase enough. Information for the yarns used for the samples is provided in the Appendix.

For all flowers, refer to the instructions on page 160 to felt the flowers as desired.

Refer to the instructions on page 32 for wiring the stem and petals. Wire the felted flowers *after* they have been felted.

The Power of Gauge
or How to Knit Flowers for Tiny Fairies and Giant Butterflies

Almost as soon as I began to knit, I learned about the mysterious power of gauge. I was asked to check it, to check it again, to swatch, and to re-swatch. You may be relieved to know that gauge is not critical for these flowers in the same way it is for, say, a sweater, for the simple reason that flowers don't have to fit when they are done. This gives us tremendous freedom! Not the freedom to ignore gauge, but an invitation to play with and understand it in a new way.

As mentioned earlier, the flowers in these pages will be most successful if they are knit densely. *Even if* you plan to felt all the flowers you knit, you should, nevertheless, knit with some compactness of stitches because this gives the flowers greater dimension and structure. When felted, densely knit flowers don't shrink so much as they lose stitch definition. In this way, two flowers worked on the same size needles, one felted and one not, may be almost exactly the same size.

While it might be easier if I said simply knit until the piece measures 3" (7.5cm), I have instead directed you to knit a certain number of rounds or rows. This is so that the flower can be scaled to any gauge, worked in any yarn without worrying about how large it should be. It would not be overstating things to say that every flower pattern can be used, just as written, to make a flower that will fit in a thimble or one so big it would need to be suspended from the rafters of a stadium. This is the power of gauge.

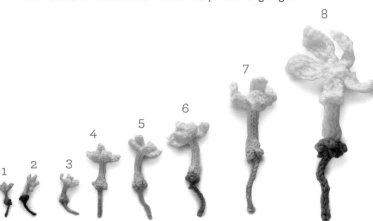

12

1. Shibui *Silk Cloud* (lace weight); size 000–000 (0.7mm) needles

2. Alpaca with a Twist *Fino* (fingering weight); size 000–00 needles (1mm) needles

3. A single ply of Stonehedge Fiber Mill *Shepherd's Wool* (fingering weight); size 0000 (1.2mm) needles

4. A single ply of Stonehedge Fiber Mill *Shepherd's Wool* (fingering weight); size 000 (1.5mm) needles

5. Stonehedge Fiber Mill *Shepherd's Wool* (fingering weight); size 00 (1.75mm) needles

6. Stonehedge Fiber Mill *Shepherd's Wool* (worsted weight); size 1 (2.25mm) needles

7. A strand of Stonehedge Fiber Mill *Shepherd's Wool* worsted weight and a strand of fingering weight; size 6 (4mm) needles

8. Universal Yarn *Deluxe Worsted* double strand; size 9 (5.5mm) needles

9. Shibui *Highland Wool Alpaca* single strand; size 11 (8mm) needles

10. Shibui *Highland Wool Alpaca* double strand; size 13 (9mm) needles

11. Shibui *Highland Wool Alpaca* quadruple strand; size 17 (12.75mm) needles

12. Stonehedge Fiber Mill *Merino Top*; size 50 needles

Anatomy of a Knitted Flower

The patterns that follow refer to floral anatomy with botanical names, so take a moment to familiarize yourself with the different parts of a flower.

As you knit from flower to flower, you may become aware that some of the flowers don't have all the parts listed here. This is because some flowers, called "perfect flowers," contain everything they need to fertilize themselves, while others, called "imperfect flowers," do not. It's interesting to note that even with all the necessary sexual parts, however, some flowers refuse to self-fertilize and reject any pollen that is too familiar.

Where it wasn't possible to refer to a specific part, I try to be as descriptive as possible.

ARTICULATION. The point where the stem narrows just below the receptacle.

CALYX. All the sepals as a unit. The calyx is the protective sheath out of which the petals emerge.

COROLLA. The petals of a flower as a group.

PEDICEL. The stem of a specific flower. If there are multiple flowers, the peduncle is the main stem off which the pedicels branch and terminate in a blossom.

PEDUNCLE. The main stem.

PETALS. The showy part of the flower that draws the attention of pollinators and gives them information about where the nectar and pollen are located.

PISTIL. The female reproductive body, made up of three main parts:

> **Stigma**. Generally located at the top of the pistil, this is the sticky part that collects pollen.

> **Style**. The long tube pollen must navigate in order to reach the stigma, where it can fertilize the ovules that reside in the ovary.

> **Ovary**. Located at the base of the pistil, this is where the pollen commingles with the ovule to make seeds. This part later swells to become the seed pod.

RECEPTACLE. The structural foundation for the flower. It is located at the top of the stem and is the place to which all parts of the flower are attached.

SEPALS. The small leaves that reside under the petals. These leaves are the protective covering (the calyx) for the flower bud.

STAMENS. The stamens are the male reproductive bodies that manufacture pollen. Each stamen consists of two parts:

> **Filament**. A narrow stalk that is topped by the anther.

> **Anther**. The knob at the end of the filament that holds the pollen.

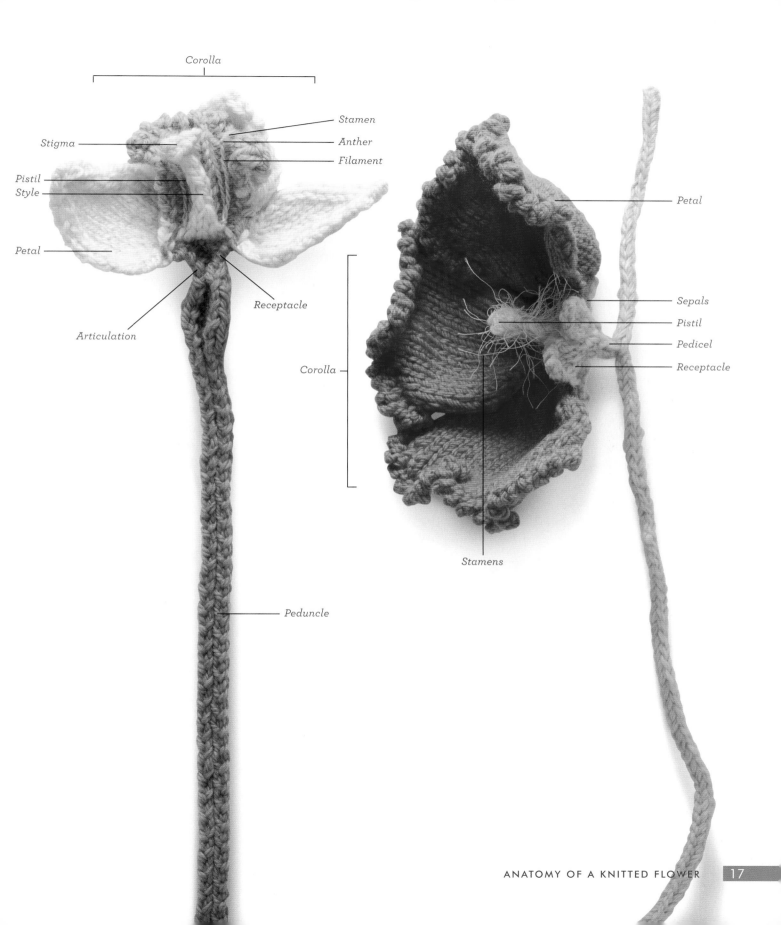

Corolla

Stamen

Stigma

Anther

Filament

Pistil

Style

Petal

Receptacle

Articulation

Corolla

Petal

Sepals

Pistil

Pedicel

Receptacle

Stamens

Peduncle

Difficulty Levels

I've come to think of knitting the flowers in this book as a journey: I began with the familiar and simpler flowers, and as my own skills were honed, I was able to create flowers of greater complexity, building detail with a set of techniques.

The flowers labeled *Starting Out* are the simplest in the book and are accessible to knitters with a sound knowledge of knitting basics. These flowers don't necessarily include the same detail that their actual flower counterparts possess, as I've simplified the patterns for greater ease of working. The subsequent difficulty levels all build on the basic techniques used in *Starting Out* and *On the Way*. In this manner, I use gauge as a sort of microscope: *Intrepid* flowers are more detailed or larger and so take more time. *Resolute* flowers have even finer detail and in some cases greater voluptuousness, which necessitates an equal delicacy of work. The ruffled petal edges of the pheasant's eye daffodil and the Shirley poppy, while not difficult, take time.

I invite you to begin this walk through the garden as I did, with the simplest flowers, studying them, appreciating their simplicity even as you develop the skills to make them more complex . . . and, so, in the manner of a bee, on to enjoy the next flower.

STARTING OUT 𝄠 𝄠 𝄠 𝄠

The knitter must know how to cast on and bind off, to perform basic knit and purl stitches, increase and decrease using methods such as knit in the front and back of a stitch and make one (without attention to slant). Most of these patterns contain minimal shaping, easy felting, easy blocking, and minimal or no finishing other than careful weaving in of ends.

ON THE WAY 𝄠 𝄠 𝄠 𝄠

These flowers and projects build on the skills needed for those labeled *Starting Out*. The knitter must be able to maintain even tension during repetitive stitch patterns and simple color changes using double-pointed needles. The patterns require simple shaping using standard directional increasing and decreasing. These flowers will require careful weaving in of ends and simple felting.

INTREPID 𝄠 𝄠 𝄠 𝄠

Knitters making these flowers and projects must be comfortable using a variety of techniques, such as short rows, simple intarsia, use of double-pointed needles and knitting-in-the-round techniques, midlevel shaping, and finishing, such as top application of flowers and floral designs, overstitching, embroidery, and some beadwork.

With regard to projects involving purses, the knitter will be asked to create tassels and to apply purse frames or other handles.

RESOLUTE 𝄠 𝄠 𝄠 𝄠

The knitter of these flowers and projects will use advanced techniques and stitches, such as short rows, detailed intarsia, numerous color changes, and intricate finishing, such as fine weaving in of ends, hand-beading, and hand-sewing.

Essential Tools

KNITTING NEEDLES
Double-Pointed Needles

Every flower in this book has one or more components that is worked in the round. For this reason, double-pointed needles are essential. If you want to make flowers of vastly differing sizes, you will need a range of different needle sizes. They come in multiple materials, but I opt for velvet-smooth bamboo and the lightness of hollow stainless steel. For very tiny flowers, stainless needles are the only option: Where wood would break, the stainless steel only bends with the work of your hands.

Conventional Straight Needles

For those who prefer conventional knitting needles, almost all petals—save perhaps the curved single petal of the calla lily—can be worked using straight needles.

Circular Needles

Larger flowers that require many stitches on hold waiting to be worked, such as the sunflower, are made much easier with a few circular needles.

SEWING/DARNING NEEDLES

Like most knitters, I have a little needle case of blunt-pointed tapestry needles always available. It wasn't until I was weaving in the ends of these flowers that I began to use sharp-pointed darning or embroidery needles *all the time*.

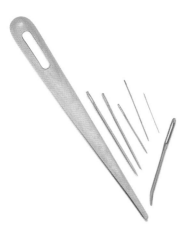

To make any number of flowers, you'll need a wide range of sharp needles: long, delicate ones for beading; slender, short ones for hand-sewing; and large-eyed needles of various sizes and lengths for weaving in ends, wiring stems and petals, and tacking petals together in realistic configurations.

TAPE MEASURE

A tape measure comes in handy if you choose to work at the sample flower gauge, so that you can check your results against mine. It's also useful as you make any of the projects.

STITCH HOLDERS

Every flower in this book will require you to put stitches on holders as you work different flower components. You can, of course, use other materials in any of these instances: I recommend wire for very tiny flowers, scrap yarn in the same gauge as the flower, or rope for larger-gauge flowers. I found locking stitch markers invaluable when working lace-, fingering-, and worsted-weight flowers. For more information about stitch holders of different sizes, refer to the section on Working Small and Large (page 27).

SCISSORS AND/OR THREAD CLIPPERS

Because many of the flowers have so many different parts, there are many ends to weave in and trim. A pair of excellent, sharp thread clippers or small scissors specifically intended for such fine work is essential. While not pictured here, hardy workhorse scissors that can cut just about anything from plastic to wire are also necessary.

BEADS

Seed beads bring some dazzle to any flower, as though the cool night had left it decorated with dew. The right contrasting color, such as red beads on the petals of an Oriental lily, can turn a Casablanca into a Stargazer. I also recommend hand-beading for many of the projects. Even a few well-placed beads can make an otherwise lovely wrap, bag, or set of gloves into a truly spectacular and completely unique statement of your creativity.

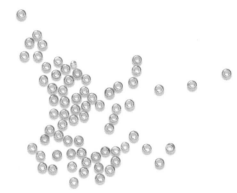

WIRE

Excellent wire for structuring flowers can be found in most craft stores or full-service bead shops. Such wire comes in various gauges and colors. I prefer 26-gauge wire for most flowers and 28-gauge wire for the more delicate, lighter-gauge blossoms. Brass wire is an excellent wire for any flower and is more economical, as it can be purchased on larger spools. Sometimes I like working with wire the same color as the stem or petals. The dark petals of the hollyhock, for example, do not betray the dark wine and black wire I used, even when the wire was close to the surface.

THREAD

I prefer polyester or nylon beading thread for any necessary hand-sewing, tacking, or beading. It's best to choose thread that's close in color to your flower or project.

Abbreviations & Special Terms

Here is a list of the abbreviations I use throughout, as well as descriptions of techniques and special terms.

3-needle bind-off. With right sides facing each other and an equal number of stitches divided between two parallel needles, *insert the tip of a third needle knitwise into the first stitch of the front needle and then knitwise into the first stitch of the back needle. Knit these two stitches together; repeat from * so there are two stitches on the right-hand needle. Pass the first stitch worked over the second so one stitch remains on the right needle and repeat this entire process until all stitches are bound off.

Backward-loop cast-on. Begin with a slip knot on the needle. Hold the needle in one hand and, *with the working yarn, make a loop and place it on the needle backward or twisted so that it does not unwind; repeat from * until the required number of stitches has been cast on.

Cable cast-on. Begin with a slip knot on the left-hand needle; knit into the slip knot, leaving the slip-knot stitch on the left needle and slipping the new stitch knitwise onto the left-hand needle. *Knit into the space between the last two stitches on the left-hand needle. Slip the new stitch knitwise onto the left-hand needle; repeat from * until the requisite number of stitches has been cast on.

cm	centimeter(s)
g	gram(s)
K	knit
k2tog	knit 2 stitches together decrease
k3tog	knit 3 stitches together decrease
kfb	knit into the front and back of a stitch increase
kfbf	knit into the front, back, and front of a stitch increase

Knitted cast-on. Begin with a slip knot on the left-hand needle; knit into the slip knot, leaving the slip knot stitch on the left needle and slipping the new stitch knitwise onto the left-hand needle. *Knit into the last stitch created and then slip the new stitch knitwise onto the left-hand needle; repeat from * until the requisite number of stitches has been cast on.

LI-L	Knit left loop increase: knit the left side of the stitch below the stitch just worked
LI-R	Knit right loop increase: knit the right side of the stitch below the stitch just worked
m	meters

mm	millimeters
M1	Make 1: increase 1 stitch using either a M1-L or a M1-R
M1-L	Make 1—left slant increase: Lift the bar between the stitches and place it over the left-hand needle from back to front. Use the right-hand needle to knit the bar through the back loop, creating a twisted stitch.
M1-P	Make 1 purl stitch: Lift the bar between the stitches and place it over the left-hand needle from back to front. Use the right-hand needle to purl the bar through the back loop, creating a twisted (purl) stitch.
M1-R	Make 1—right slant increase: Lift the bar between the stitches and place it over the left-hand needle from front to back. Use the right-hand needle to knit the bar through the front loop creating a twisted stitch.
oz	ounce(s)
p	purl
p2tog	purl 2 stitches together
p3tog	purl 3 stitches together

pfb	purl in the front and back of a stitch		

pfb purl in the front and back of a stitch

psso pass slipped stitch over the last stitch worked

sBO Sewn bind-off: Cut the yarn, leaving a long tail (approximately 3 times the length of the piece being bound off). With the right side of the work facing you and using a tapestry needle, *insert the needle through the first 2 stitches as if to purl and then back through the first stitch as if to

knit and take the first stitch off the needle. Repeat from * until all stitches are bound off.

skp slip 1, knit 1, pass slipped stitch over

sk2p slip 1, k2tog, pass slipped stitch over

sl 1 slip 1 stitch

ssk slip 2 stitches 1 at a time knitwise, then k2tog-tbl

ssp slip 2 stitches 1 at a time knitwise, then pass back to the left-hand needle; p2tog-tbl

sssk slip 3 stitches 1 at a time knitwise, then k3tog-tbl

sssp slip 3 stitches 1 at a time knitwise, then pass those stitches back to the left-hand needle; p3tog-tbl

tbl through the back of the loop

W&T wrap and turn (for short rows)

yb with the yarn in back

yds yards

yfw with the yarn in front

yo yarn over

CYCA Standard Yarn Weights

YARN WEIGHT SYMBOL AND CATEGORY NAMES	0 lace	1 super fine	2 fine	3 light	4 medium	5 bulky	6 super bulky
TYPE OF YARNS IN CATEGORY	Fingering 10-count crochet thread	Sock, Fingering, Baby	Sport, Baby	DK, Light Worsted	Worsted, Afghan, Aran	Chunky, Craft, Rug	Bulky, Roving
KNIT GAUGE RANGE* IN STOCKINETTE TO 4"	33–40**sts	27–32 sts	23–26 sts	21–24 sts	16–20 sts	12–15 sts	6–11 sts
RECOMMENDED NEEDLE SIZE, METRIC	1.5–2.25mm	2.25–3.25mm	3.25–3.75mm	3.75–4.5mm	4.5–5.5mm	5.5–8mm	8mm and larger
RECOMMENDED NEEDLE SIZE, U.S.	000–1	1–3	3–5	5–7	7–9	9–11	11 and larger

* Please note that these are GUIDELINES ONLY based on the most commonly used gauges and needle or hook sizes for specific yarn categories.

** Lace-weight yarns are usually worked on larger needles to create lacy, openwork patterns. Accordingly, a gauge range is difficult to determine. Always follow the gauge stated in your pattern.

Special Techniques

As I worked on developing these flower patterns, I used several specialized techniques over and over. If you don't understand these techniques, the patterns may cause moments of confusion. For best results, read through these techniques, and practice them a few times simply to perfect your skills so that working the flowers themselves goes smoothly. There may be instances when what I ask you to do in a particular pattern might feel awkward; in these instances, I've tried to note that such awkwardness is to be expected.

WORKING IN THE ROUND: I-CORD STEMS OF DIFFERENT SIZES

2-to-5-stitch I-cord

1   Cast on 5 stitches.

2   Knit the 5 stitches (stitches are now on the left end of a double-pointed needle).

3   Without turning the work, slip the 5 stitches to the other end of the double-pointed needle and knit. Repeat these steps until the requisite number of rounds is achieved.

6-or-more-stitch I-cord

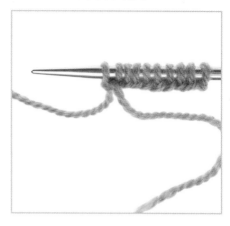

1   Cast on 10 stitches.

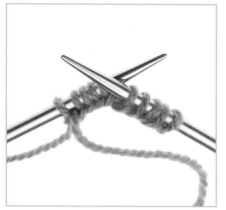

2   Divide the stitches between 2 double-pointed needles.

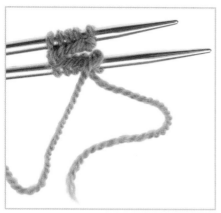

3   Position the needles so that they are parallel, with the wrong sides facing each other. Slip the stitches to the right-hand ends of both needles; as pictured, the live yarn should come from the back needle.

4   Knit the stitches on the "first" (front) needle using the live yarn and a third needle. Turn both needles around so, again, the live yarn is coming from the back needle and knit the stitches on the second needle.

5   Repeat these steps until the requisite number of rounds is achieved.

The stems and receptacles for these flowers—that is, all the setup for the sepal leaves and petals—are worked in the round. Most of the flowers will require that you knit with multiple colors in particular rounds in order to, for example, set up the stitches for the sepal leaves, the petals, the stamens, and the pistil all at the same time. For best results, it is imperative that the different colors or multiple strands of the same color be kept in the same relative order in each stitch.

Divide the stitches onto different holders for ease of working

There are many instances in which stitches will need to be slipped onto holders as they wait to be worked. As you embark on a particular flower, make sure you have materials that will work as appropriate holders.

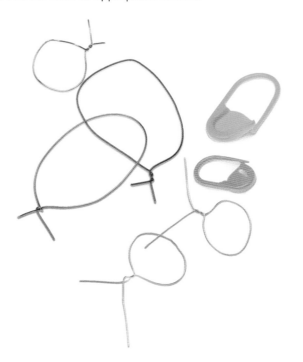

Small Flowers

Flowers worked with lace-weight or thread-weight yarn on tiny needles can't accommodate standard locking stitch markers. Make your own holders from 28-gauge wire cut into 1" (2.5cm) lengths and twisted together at the ends to hold the stitches. I don't recommend using scrap yarn, as you may need a magnifying glass to pick up the stitches again—I speak from experience.

True-to-Life Flowers (fingering- and worsted-weight)

Use small-sized conventional locking stitch markers or scrap yarn as holders for fingering-, light worsted–, and worsted-weight yarns. For slightly larger flowers, made from a double-strand of worsted-weight yarn, you may use the large-sized conventional locking stitch markers. It's very easy to slip stitches on and off these markers.

Giant Flowers

Conventional sweater or even afghan stitch holders work very well for giant flowers. If you are daring enough to make humungous flowers, you might need to resort to using scrap yarn: In this case, I recommend lengths of cotton and other slick-fiber-content yarns or slick rope as holders.

WEAVING IN ENDS FOR BEST RESULTS

Use a Darning Needle for a Better "Stick"
Because these flowers are intended to be beautiful, whether or not they are felted, it is crucial that woven-in ends stay put. The sharpness of the darning needle point splits the yarn fibers so that your end goes through existing strands of yarn, rather than under or over, and is, therefore, more likely to stay where you intend.

Weave in at Least 1" (2.5cm)
Whether or not you're felting, short ends are more likely to come undone and poke out in the least-wanted places. The solution is to weave in at least 1" (2.5cm) and more if you can. This is perhaps even more important for flowers that will be felted. Ends that undo themselves can cause your flowers to unravel in the wash. Take the time to avoid this.

CAREFULLY CHOOSE WHERE TO WEAVE IN AN END

Please use the following guidelines when weaving ends into any flower, whether or not you intend to felt it:

Weave in along Underside Edges

Weave in along underside edges so that the weave-in is as unobtrusive as possible.

Weave Ends into Matching Color Fields

When working with color intersections, it's best to secure the intersections with a square knot (right over left, left over right) and then weave the different colors into their respective color fields. If you're changing colors either through striping or intarsia, weave ends into same-color field edges, even if you must work horizontally, to make them as invisible as possible.

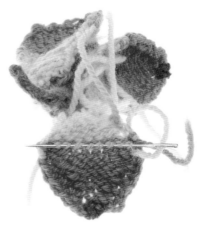

Weave in an End by Tacking or Drawing Flower Components Together

There are times when flower petals lie on top of each other in particular ways—the large upper petals of the pansy, for example. Tails can be used to tack the petals into these particular configurations.

Tails can also be used to give greater structure to stamens. For example, the stamens of the crocus and star magnolia benefit from ends being woven in at the base of the stamens to help them stand upright.

Use the Weaving-in Process as a Way to Strengthen Delicate Intersections

Weave in petal tails by taking a small stitch in the receptacle before weaving in the end on the petal underside. This strengthens the articulation between the petal and receptacle.

MAKING STAMENS

Some flowers include stamens as part of the pattern. The crocus and Oriental lily are good examples. Below is a technique I developed to replicate the delicate, fringelike stamens by using lighter-gauge yarns. A caveat: If you wish to felt the flowers, make stamens *after* felting.

   You'll need scissors or thread clippers, a number of lengths of the specified lighter-gauge yarn, a sharp needle, and fabric glue.

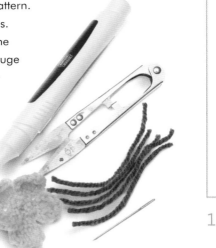

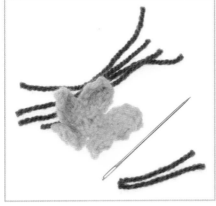

1   *Fold one strand in half to make a loop.

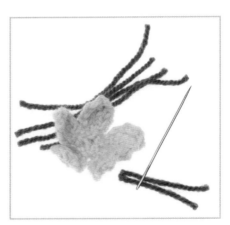

2   Thread the loop on a sharp darning needle.

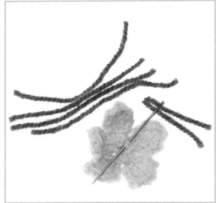

3   Insert the needle into the base of the pistil or the area just outside the flower center, making sure the needle is pointed toward the center. This orientation helps the yarn stand up as stamens do.

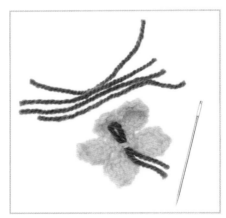

4   Use the darning needle to draw the folded end through the knitted fabric at the center.

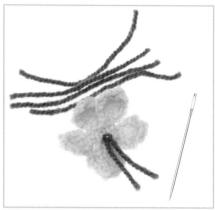

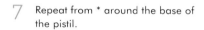

5   Open the loop and pull the loose ends through the loop.

6   Draw the knot up firmly.

7   Repeat from * around the base of the pistil.

8   Tie a small overhand knot in each strand about ½" (13mm) from the stamen base, at the height specified in the pattern, or at an appropriate height for the gauge flower you are making.

9   Dot each knot with fabric or craft glue.

10   Trim the strands to just above the knot.

WIRING STEMS AND BLOSSOMS: AN OVERVIEW AND BASIC METHOD

Most flowers in this book will benefit from wired stems and petals. Before wiring, unfortunately, most flowers curl up.

There are some general rules of thumb to help you decide whether or not to wire. For felted flowers, wire after felting while the flower is still slightly damp; this allows the wire to move more smoothly through the felted fabric and the felt to be more easily molded. Felting gives any flower more structure, so wiring is not as important as it would be otherwise; however, wiring gives even the felted flower greater dimension and keeps it shaped the way you want it. Once the tulip is felted, for example, its petals flatten out, rather than curling up like an exotic pastry, but the petals will not stay oriented in a tulip-like manner, nor will they maintain a cupped shape unless assisted by wire.

Smaller flowers are the least likely to need wiring—a worsted-weight periwinkle changes little with wiring. It will, nevertheless, stand up on its own in a small vase if you wire its stem.

In short, wiring makes these flowers come alive, and when they are well-wired, they will amaze you with just how likely they are to fool you.

The wired flowers in this book use 26- or 28-gauge beading wire in brass or a desired color. The result is a flower that has a good deal of structure and will maintain its shape if sewn to a hatband or a garment, or tied to a gift box. If you want your large flowers to stand up in a vase, you will need to use a heavier-gauge wire. Because heavier-gauge wire is also harder to work with, you may want to knit your stems and flower petals around the wire. This presents problems, however, if and when you want to felt the flowers, so it is a technique best used for flowers you will not felt.

For large flowers with stems that are 8-stitch or more, you can insert a dowel in the stem to help it stand up.

Materials you will need for basic wiring of stems and petals: 28- or 26-gauge beading wire in brass or desired color, a large-eyed sharp needle, and a pair of sturdy scissors with which to cut wire.

1   Measure out a strand of wire that is 1 yard (1m) long. Thread the wire on your needle.

2   *Insert the needle into the bottom of the stem or the petal edge and travel through the knitted or felted fabric.

3   Avoid letting the needle "surface" and so expose the wire on the outside of the flower.

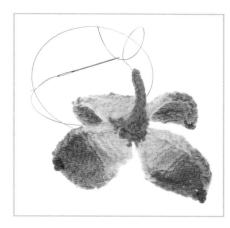

4 Bring the needle out of the flower fabric in order to pull the wire snug, just as you would pull thread tight when making a running stitch.

5 Caution: The wire will try to twist and kink as you pull it tight.

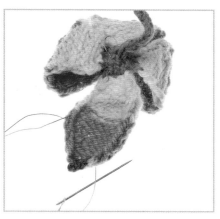

6 Remedy a kink-in-the-making by twisting the wire into a U shape as you pull tight.

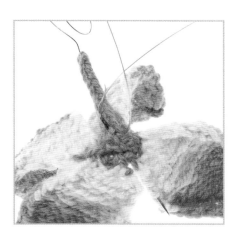

7 Once the wire is pulled snug (but not so tight as to distort the flower), insert the needle back in where it came out.

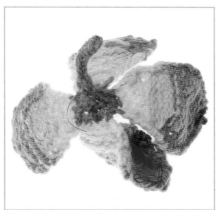

8 Repeat from * until a particular portion of the flower is completely wired. Caution: It is best to end wiring at a natural location, such as the top of the stem or the intersection of petal with receptacle. Then cut the wire end flush with the flower.

9 The wired flower has structure and can be molded into its characteristic growth habit.

The Flowers

As I worked on these flowers, I examined real flowers from every angle, read about the habits of plants, learned about how they got their names, and pored over the history that surrounds them: The introduction of the tulip to Europe in the early 1600s, for example, resulted in the first real economic "bubble" when the prices for tulip bulbs reached extraordinary highs. This is only one tiny historical tidbit.

More compelling even than the history of the flower is each flower itself. My objective was to understand the actual flower, its roots, bulb, leaf, peduncle, pedicel, sepal, flower. Only then could it be knitted. Inspired by botanicals, where each aspect of a plant is lovingly detailed, I photographed these knitted flowers with their real-life foliage whenever possible. Over the course of working on this project, I have come to see flowers in a new way. It was only after I had made the crocus sample for the book that my own crocuses came up and I discovered that their stems are not green, but white, purple, or striated in the two colors. I am continually amazed by the secret life of flowers. To design their forms as knitted structures was to grapple with their details. And their details are not only gorgeous but stunningly physical, even sexual: The sole purpose of the flower is reproduction. When this work is done, the flower dies. Plants store up their energy in order to dazzle pollinators with their scents and their fantastic displays. They are not passive bystanders but actively call bees or beetles or butterflies to their blossoms. Their painted or speckled throats are invitations, their scents are promises, their structures are purposeful.

If you study a flower's details, you may notice that I haven't always accurately represented them, occasionally because I wanted to focus on a certain simplicity of line and structure, and sometimes because an accurately detailed representation would be impossible without increasing the scale of the flower. Showing the tiny petals, pistil, and stamens at the center of the dogwood calyx, for example, would necessitate a flower the size of a platter. But simply noticing such a deficiency of detail has a certain sweetness. I want you to notice. I want you to note the way the Oriental lily has three large petals, three small, and the swirl of them at their base when the flower has just opened. I want you to get down and peer into the throat of a single foxglove flower—and to wonder how to knit it.

Angel's
Tears
Daffodil

Narcissus triandrus

DIFFICULTY LEVEL 𝟈 𝟈 𝟈 𝟈

REQUIRED YARN COLORS

Green (A), pale pink (B), pink or pale peach (C), and lighter-gauge yarn in yellow (D)

SAMPLE

Finished Measurements

Flower head diameter: 2" (5cm)
Stem length: 10" (25.5cm)

Yarns Used

Stonehedge Fiber Mill *Shepherd's Wool* (worsted weight) Lime (A), Baby Pink (B), Pink (C), and (fingering weight) Spring Chick (D)

PATTERN NOTE

Requires needles approximately 5 sizes smaller for the pistil.

INSTRUCTIONS

PEDUNCLE (MAIN STEM)

With A, cast on 5 stitches.

Work as an I-cord using the following method:

*K5, pull yarn across the back and, without turning your work, slip the row to the other end of the needle; repeat from * for 36 rounds or desired length.

Next round: K2, ssk, k1—4 stitches.

Continue to work as an I-cord for 12 more rounds.

Next round: Ssk, k2—3 stitches.

Continue to work as an I-cord for 6 more rounds.

Next round (setup stitches for pedicel [branching stem] and blossom): Kfb 3 times—6 stitches.

Next round: Keep the last 3 stitches worked on the needle. Transfer the remaining 3 stitches onto a holder unworked—3 stitches.

Continue to work the peduncle as an I-cord for 6 more rounds.

*

RECEPTACLE (FLOWER FOUNDATION)

Round 1: Kfb in each stitch—6 stitches. Divide the stitches between 2 needles.

Rounds 2–5: Knit around.

Round 6: [K1, k2tog] twice—4 stitches.

Round 7: Change to C and knit around.

Round 8: K1, M1-R, k2, M1-L, k1—6 stitches.

Rounds 9–16: Knit around.

Round 17: K3, M1, k3—7 stitches.

Rounds 18 and 19: Knit around.

Round 20: K2, M1, k5—8 stitches.

Round 21: [K1, M1-R, k2, M1-L, k1] twice—12 stitches.

Round 22: With B, C, and D held together, knit around.

Transfer the B stitches in groupings of 2 to holders held to the outside for the petals. Cut B and weave in the end.

Transfer the D stitches to 3 smaller needles held to center for the pistil.

Transfer the C stitches to 2 holders held between the outside B stitches and the center D stitches for center flute.

PISTIL

Round 1: With the live strand of D and the smaller needles, knit around.

Round 2: K2tog around—6 stitches. Divide the stitches between 2 needles.

Round 3: Knit around.

Round 4: K2tog around—3 stitches.

Rounds 5–24: Knit as for an I-cord. The objective here is to make the pistil long enough to show just beneath the narcissus flute, so if more rounds need to be worked once the flute is finished, feel free to do so.

Round 25: *Without turning your work, use the backwards-loop cast-on method to cast on 2 stitches, bind off 3. Transfer the remaining stitch to the left-hand needle and repeat from * twice more. Cut the yarn and draw through the remaining stitch. Weave in the end down the center of the pistil so that the 1st and 3rd nodes of the stigma sit snugly next to each other.

*

CENTER FLUTE

Transfer the 12 C stitches to the 2 larger needles.

Round 1: Position the flower so the peduncle is facing you. With the live strand of C, knit around.

Round 2: [K2, M1-R, k2, M1-L, k2] twice—16 stitches.

Round 3: Knit around.

Round 4: [K2, M1-R, k4, M1-L, k2] twice—20 stitches.

Rounds 5–12: Knit around.

Round 13: Bind off all stitches knitwise.

1ST PETAL

Transfer 2 B stitches to a larger needle, positioning the flower so that the center flute is facing you and the peduncle is facing away. Join a new strand of B.

Row 1 (RS): Kfbf twice—6 stitches.

Row 2 and all WS rows: Purl.

Row 3: Kfb, k4, kfb—8 stitches.

Row 5: Kfb, k6, kfb—10 stitches.

Rows 6–10: Work in stockinette stitch.

Row 11: K1, ssk, k4, k2tog, k1—8 stitches.

Row 13: K1, ssk, k2, k2tog, k1—6 stitches.

Row 15: K1, ssk, k2tog, k1—4 stitches.

Row 17: Ssk, k2tog and *at the same time* bind off. Cut the yarn and pull the tail through the remaining stitch. Weave in the ends along the petal's underside edge.

*

2ND & SUBSEQUENT PETALS

Transfer the 2 stitches to the left of the petal just worked to a larger needle. Join a new strand of B and repeat rows 1–17. Continue in this manner until all 6 petals are complete. Weave in ends at the base and apex of each petal.

*

2ND FLOWER

Transfer the 3 stitches for the pedicel (branching stem) to a larger needle. Join a new strand of A and work as an I-cord for 12 rounds. Complete as

for the 1st flower, beginning with the receptacle and proceeding through to the petals.

*

STAMENS

Make 6 stamens: Cut three 6" (15cm) strands of D. Make 6 filaments according to the instructions on page 30 for making stamens. Make sure the knot that replicates the anther is just visible beneath the flute but slightly shorter than the pistil.

FINISHING

For best results, wire the peduncle and petals.

Black-Eyed Susan

Rudbeckia hirta

DIFFICULTY LEVEL 🖋🖋🖋🖋

REQUIRED YARN COLORS
Green (A), brown (B), and yellow (C)

SAMPLE
Finished Measurements
Flower head diameter: 4" (10cm)
Stem length: 16" (40.5cm)

Yarns Used
Stonehedge Fiber Mill *Shepherd's Wool* (worsted weight) Lime (A), Brown (B), and Sun Yellow (C)

INSTRUCTIONS

PEDUNCLE (MAIN STEM)
With A, cast on 2 stitches.
I-Cord Round: Knit across; without turning your work, slip the row to the other end of the needle; pull the yarn across the back to begin the next round.
Repeat the I-cord round for 24 rounds or desired length.

∗

RECEPTACLE (FLOWER FOUNDATION)
Round 1: With A, kfbf across—6 stitches.
Divide the stitches onto 2 needles; mark the beginning of the round.
Round 2: Knit around.
Round 3: [Kfb] 3 times, kfb, kfbf, kfb—13 stitches.
Round 4: Join B and C. With A, B, and C held together, knit around. Transfer the 13 B stitches to 4

double-pointed needles (distributed 4-3-3-3) held to the center for the flower center; transfer the 13 C stitches to 3 holders held between the B and A stitches for the petals; transfer the 13 A stitches to 3 holders held to the outside for the sepal leaves. Do not cut the yarns.

∗

FLOWER CENTER
Rounds 1–3: Mark the beginning of the round; knit around.
Round 4: K1, [k1, k2tog] 4 times—9 stitches.
Round 5: Knit.
Round 6: K1, [k2tog] 4 times—5 stitches.
Cut the yarn and pull the end through the remaining 5 stitches. Secure and weave the end to the inside.

∗

SEPAL LEAVES
Slip the 13 A stitches onto 3 needles.
Bind-off Round: Using a cable cast-on method, *cast on 3 stitches, then bind off 4 stitches; slip the remaining stitch from the right-hand to the left-hand needle; repeat from * until all stitches are bound off. Cut the yarn and weave in the ends so that the first and last stitch of the round sit snugly next to each other.

PETALS
Slip the 13 C stitches onto 3 double-pointed needles.
*Using a backwards-loop cast-on method, cast 13 stitches onto the left-hand needle.
Bind off the 13 stitches—1 stitch remains on the right-hand needle.
Slip 1 stitch onto the right-hand needle and bind off the 1st stitch by passing it over the slipped stitch.
Slip the remaining stitch back onto the left-hand needle.
Repeat from * until all 13 stitches are bound off, then fasten off the last stitch and weave in the end.

Bloodroot

Sanguinaria canadensis

DIFFICULTY LEVEL 🖊🖊🖊🖊

REQUIRED YARN COLORS
Mint green (A), white (B), and lighter-
gauge yarn in yellow (C)

SAMPLE
Finished Measurements
Flower head diameter: 4½" (11.5cm)
from tip to tip of largest petals
Stem length: 5" (12.5cm)

Yarns Used
Stonehedge Fiber Mill *Shepherd's
Wool* (worsted weight) Mint (A)
and White (B) and (fingering weight)
Sun Yellow (C)

PEDUNCLE (MAIN STEM)

With A, cast on 3 stitches.

I-Cord Round: Knit across; without turning your work, slip the row to the other end of the needle; pull the yarn across the back to begin the next round.

Repeat the I-cord round for 24 rounds or desired length.

*

RECEPTACLE (FLOWER FOUNDATION)

Round 1: Kfb in each stitch—6 stitches. Divide between 2 needles.

Round 2: Join a strand of B; with A and B held together, knit around. Transfer the 6 A stitches onto a holder held to center for the pistil; slip the 6 B stitches onto 2 double-pointed needles held to the outside of center A stitches to continue the receptacle. Do not cut yarns but move the strand of A to the center to work the pistil.

Round 3: With B, kfbf 6 times—18 stitches.

Round 4: Purl around.

*

PETALS

Note: Bloodroot flowers are formed by two crosses, one with 4 larger petals and the other with 4 smaller petals. Then there are one or two petals that look as though they were just stuck in as an afterthought. They're very funny, and I've included one of them here; it should be worked as a small petal.

With the center facing, keep the last 2 stitches worked during round 5 on the needle to work the 1st (small odd) petal. Transfer the remaining 16 stitches to 8 holders in 2 different colors (2 stitches on each), alternating the color of the holders for each set of stitches.

1st Small Petal

Row 1 (RS): With the live strand of B, k1, M1, k1—3 stitches.

Rows 2–4: Work in stockinette stitch.

Row 5: K1, M1-R, k1, M1-L, k1—5 stitches.

Rows 6–8: Work in stockinette stitch.

Row 9: K1, ssk, k2—4 stitches.

Row 10: P4

Row 11: Ssk, k2tog—2 stitches.

Row 12: P2.

Cut the yarn and draw the tail through the remaining 2 stitches to fasten off. Weave in the ends on the underside edge of the petal.

1st Large Petal

Transfer the 2 stitches to the left of the petal just completed to a needle.

Row 1 (RS): Join a new strand of B; k1, M1, k1—3 stitches.

Row 2: P3.

Row 3: K1, kfb, k1—4 stitches.

Row 4: P4.

Row 5: K1, M1-R, k2, M1-L, k1—6 stitches.

Rows 6–12: Work in stockinette stitch.

Row 13: Ssk, k2, k2tog—4 stitches.

Row 14: P4.

Row 15: K1, skp, k1—3 stitches.

Row 16: P3.

Row 17: Sk2p—1 stitch.

Cut the yarn and draw the tail through the remaining stitch to fasten off. Weave in the ends at the base and apex of the petal along the underside edges of the petal.

3rd–9th Petals

Transfer the 2 stitches to the left of the petal just completed to a needle. Join a new strand of B. Work a small petal, then alternate working large and small petals, ending with a small petal—4 large petals and 5 small petals.

*

PISTIL

Transfer the 6 center A stitches to a needle.

Round 1: Using the live strand of A and working as for an I-cord, k2tog 3 times—3 stitches.

Rounds 2 and 3: Knit around.

Cut the yarn and draw the tail through the remaining 3 stitches to fasten off. Weave the end down into the center to secure.

*

STAMENS

Cut 10 strands of C 3" (7.5cm) long, or an appropriately scaled length. For instructions on making stamens refer to page 30. Trim the strands so that their ends are even with apex of the flower pistil.

Cherry
Blossom

Prunus serrulata

DIFFICULTY LEVEL 🥚 🥚 🥚

REQUIRED YARN COLORS
Natural or Pale Pink (A), and lighter-gauge yarn in brown (B)

SAMPLE
Finished Measurements
Flower head diameter: 2" (5cm)

Yarns Used
Alpaca with a Twist *Baby Twist* Natural #0100 (A) or Tilli Tomas *Flurries* Natural (A), and Stonehedge Fiber Mill *Shepherd's Wool* (fingering weight) Milk Chocolate (B)

INSTRUCTIONS

RECEPTACLE (FLOWER FOUNDATION)

With a strand of A, cast on 3 stitches.

Round 1 (I-cord): Knit across; without turning your work, slip the row to the other end of the needle; pull the yarn across the back to begin the next round.

Round 2: Knit around.

Round 3: Continuing in I-cord fashion as for the first 2 rounds, k1, M1-R, k1, M1-L, k1—5 stitches.

Round 4: Working in I-cord fashion, kfb in each stitch, but do not slip the row to the other end of the needle—10 stitches. Divide stitches between 2 needles.

Round 5: Purl around. Cut the yarn and weave in the end so that the beginning and end of the round are snugly joined to one another.

1ST PETAL

Keep 2 stitches on a needle. Transfer the remaining 8 stitches to holders in groups of 2. Position the flower so that the tiny I-cord receptacle is facing away from you and the concave flower center is facing you.

Row 1 (RS): Join a new strand of A and k1, M1, k1—3 stitches.

Row 2: Purl.

Row 3: K1, M1, k1, M1, k1—5 stitches.

Row 4: Purl.

Row 5: Knit.

Row 6: Purl.

Row 7: Ssk, k1, k2tog—3 stitches.

Row 8: Without turning your work, pull the 2nd and the 3rd stitches over the 1st.

Cut the yarn and pull the tail through the remaining stitch to fasten off. Use a darning needle to weave in the ends along petal underside edges.

✳

2ND–5TH PETALS

Transfer the 2 stitches immediately to the left of the petal you have just made to a needle to work the next petal. Join a new strand of A and complete as for the 1st petal.

✳

FINISHING

When making worsted-weight or smaller-sized flowers, I found it was *not* necessary to wire the petals.

STAMENS

For each flower, cut 4 strands of B 3" (7.5cm) long, adjusting the strand length for smaller- or larger-gauge flowers. For instructions on making stamens, refer to page 30. Trim the strands to approximately ⅕" (5mm) or an appropriately scaled length.

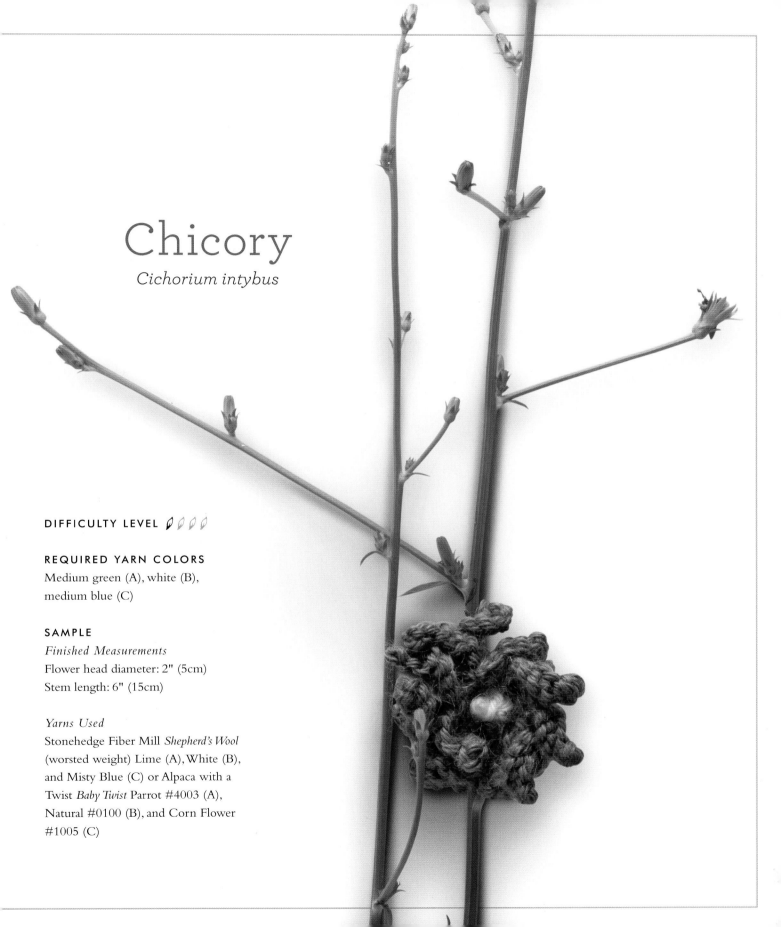

Chicory

Cichorium intybus

DIFFICULTY LEVEL ✿✿✿✿

REQUIRED YARN COLORS
Medium green (A), white (B),
medium blue (C)

SAMPLE
Finished Measurements
Flower head diameter: 2" (5cm)
Stem length: 6" (15cm)

Yarns Used
Stonehedge Fiber Mill *Shepherd's Wool*
(worsted weight) Lime (A), White (B),
and Misty Blue (C) or Alpaca with a
Twist *Baby Twist* Parrot #4003 (A),
Natural #0100 (B), and Corn Flower
#1005 (C)

PEDUNCLE
(MAIN STEM)

With A, cast on 2 stitches.

I-Cord Round: Knit across; without turning your work, slip the row to the other end of the needle; pull the yarn across the back to begin the next round.

Repeat the I-cord round for 12 rounds or desired length.

❋

RECEPTACLE
(FLOWER FOUNDATION)

Round 1: K1, M1, k1—3 stitches.

Round 2: Join a strand of B; with A and B held together, knit around. Transfer the 3 B stitches to a needle held to the center for the pistil. Transfer the 3 A stitches to 2 holders held to the outside to continue the receptacle. Do not cut the yarns.

❋

PISTIL

With the live strand of B, work 2 rounds as an I-cord.

Cut B and draw the tail through the 3 stitches to fasten off. Pull tight and secure the tail inside the pistil.

❋

RECEPTACLE
(CONTINUED)

Transfer the 3 A stitches to a needle.

Round 3: With the live strand of A kfb, k1, kfb—5 stitches. It will feel a bit awkward, but work the receptacle around the pistil. Divide the stitches between 2 needles, 1 on each side of the pistil.

Round 4: Join a strand of C; with A and C held together, knit around. Slip the 5 C stitches onto 2 holders for the petals; transfer the 5 A stitches to 2 needles held to the outside for the sepal leaves. Hold the live strand of C to the center to work the petals.

❋

SEPAL LEAVES

With the peduncle facing you, transfer the 5 sepal (A) stitches to 3 needles (arranged 1-2-2), putting the stitch to the left of the live yarn on its own needle.

Bind-off Round: Beginning with the single stitch, use a backwards-loop cast-on method to *cast 3 stitches onto the needle. Bind off the 3 cast-on stitches—1 stitch remains on the right-hand needle. Slip the next stitch from the left-hand needle (holding 2 stitches) onto the right-hand needle and bind off the 1st stitch by passing it over the slipped stitch. Slip the remaining stitch back onto the left-hand needle. Repeat from * until all 5 sepal stitches are bound off, then cut the yarn and fasten off the last stitch. Weave in the end so that the sepal leaves are placed evenly around the top of the peduncle/receptacle of the flower.

PETALS

Transfer the 5 C stitches to 2 needles.

Round 1: With the live strand of C, kfbf 5 times—15 stitches. Divide the stitches between 3 needles.

Bind-off Row: Using the backwards-loop cast-on method and C, *cast on 7 stitches and bind off 8 stitches; slip the remaining stitch from the right-hand needle onto the left-hand needle; repeat from * until all 15 stitches have been bound off—15 petals. Cut the yarn, leaving a long tail. Using the live yarn and a sharp needle, weave in the ends so that the petals sit snugly around the pistil, the first and last petal next to each other. Tack the sepal leaves to the underside of the petals.

Chionodoxa

Chionodoxa forbesii
'Glory of the Snow'

DIFFICULTY LEVEL 𝆕 𝆕 𝆕 𝆕

REQUIRED YARN COLORS

Green (A), white (B), pale blue or pink (C), and pale yellow (D)

SAMPLES

Finished Measurements

Flower head diameter: 2½" (6.5cm)

Stem length: 5¼" (13.5cm)

Yarns Used

Stonehedge Fiber Mill *Shepherd's Wool* (fingering weight) Lime Green (A), White (B), Misty Blue (C), and Spring Chick (D)

INSTRUCTIONS

PEDUNCLE (MAIN STEM) & PEDICELS (BRANCHING STEMS)

With A, cast on 3 stitches.

I-Cord Round: Knit across; without turning your work, slip the row to the other end of the needle; pull the yarn across the back to begin the next round.

Repeat the I-cord round for 36 rounds or desired length.

Setup round for 1st pedicel: [Kfb] twice, k1—5 stitches.

Next round: K5; slip the first 2 stitches onto a holder to be worked later and keep the next 3 on the needle.

Work 10 I-cord rounds.

Setup round for 2nd pedicel: K1, [kfb] twice—5 stitches.

Next round: K5; keep the first 3 stitches on the needle and slip the next 2 stitches onto a holder to be worked later.

Continue working 3-stitch I-cord for an additional 12 rounds. Cut A. If desired, more blossoms may be added by repeating the process outlined above for creating additional pedicels, working 5–12 rounds between each pedicel.

*

RECEPTACLE (FLOWER FOUNDATION) FOR MAIN FLOWER

Round 1: Change to B; k3. Tie the tails of A and B together in a square knot and weave A down the peduncle. Weave B in later into the receptacle.

Round 2: Kfb in each stitch—6 stitches.

Divide the stitches between 2 needles.

Round 3: [Kfbf, kfb, kfbf] twice—16 stitches.

Round 4: [K2, slip 1 stitch unworked onto a holder and hold to the center, k2, slip 1 stitch unworked onto the holder at center, k2] twice—12 stitches remain on the needles with 4 stitches on a holder for the flower center.

Round 5: Purl around. Cut B and weave the end into the receptacle.

*

1ST PETAL

Position the flower so that the center of the flower is facing toward you and the peduncle is facing away; keep the last 2 stitches worked in round 5 on a needle and transfer the remaining 10 stitches to holders.

———————— TIP ————————

If you are working with very small yarn, as I was for the samples, you may want to put all 10 stitches on 1 small holder for greater ease of working.

Row 1 (RS): Join a strand of C; k1, M1, k1—3 stitches.

Row 2: P1, k1, p1.

Row 3: k1, M1, p1, M1, k1—5 stitches.

Row 4: P2, k1, p2.

Rows 5–14: Work in established stitch pattern.

Row 15: Ssk, k1, k2tog—3 stitches.

Row 16: P3.

Row 17: Sk2p—1 stitch.

Cut the yarn and draw the end through the remaining stitch. Weave in the ends along the petal underside edges.

*

2ND–6TH PETALS

Transfer the 2 stitches to the left of the petal just completed to a needle.

Join a new strand of C and work as for 1st petal.

As I was weaving in petal ends,
I used one of the strands from the
base of a single petal to draw the
base of every petal together to form
a bit of a cup shape right above the
field of B. Once all the petals were
drawn snugly together at that point,
I wove in the end I was working
with to secure the shape.

STAMENS

Transfer the 4 stitches on the center
holder to 2 needles (the needles
should be parallel).
Rounds 1–3: Join a strand of B; knit
around.
Cut the yarn, draw the tail through
the remaining 4 stitches, and weave
the end down the peduncle so that it
is invisible.

*

PISTIL

To replicate the pistil in the flower
center, use a tapestry needle to thread
a strand of D up through a bit of the
peduncle and the receptacle from the
underside. Position the end so that it is
sticking out of the flower center slightly.
Tie an overhand knot in the strand so
that the knot is positioned just above
the ends of the stamens (keep the
needle on the strand as you do this);
then make a tiny invisible stitch at the
top of the stamens to secure the knot
in place there, and thread the tail end
back down through the flower center
and into the peduncle to finish off.
Cut off any excess end bits.

PEDICELS
(BRANCHING STEMS)
1st Pedicel
(2 stitches closest to the main flower)

Transfer the 2 stitches to a needle.
Round 1: Join a strand of A; k1, M1,
k1—3 stitches.
Continue as a 3-stitch I-cord until
the piece is slightly shorter than the
peduncle.
Beginning with the foundation for petals, work a flower in the same manner as the flower on the peduncle.

2nd Pedicel
*(2 stitches farthest away
from the main flower)*

Transfer the 2 stitches to a needle and
work as for the 1st pedicel, continuing
as an I-cord until the piece reaches
about halfway to the main flower.
Work the flower in the same manner
as the flower on the peduncle.

FINISHING

Arrange the petals so that 3 petals are
brought to the fore, while 3 petals are
somewhat recessed. Use like-colored
sewing thread and a sharp needle to
tack petals together. If you are wiring
petals, tack them together after completing the wiring process and bend
them so that petals curve gently up
and then downward at the tips.

Clematis
Clematis niobe

DIFFICULTY LEVEL ◊◊◊◊

REQUIRED YARN COLORS
Green (A), natural white/cream (B)
magenta (C), lighter magenta or red
(D), and Crystal Palace *Fizz* (if not
available, you'll need some kind of
short, textured, eyelash-type yarn) in
white (E)

SAMPLE
Finished Measurements
Flower head diameter: 10" (25.5cm)
Short stem length: 4" (10cm)

Yarns Used
Nashua Handknits *Julia* Spring Green
#5185 (A), Natural #0010 (B), Zinnia
Pink #5084 (C), and Geranium #6085
(D)
Crystal Palace *Fizz* White #7300 (E)

PATTERN NOTES
• Petals are worked using the intarsia
  method, bringing the next color
  from below the previous color to interlock the yarns and prevent holes.
• When working across short rows,
  there's no need to hide the wraps.

PEDUNCLE (MAIN STEM)

With A, cast on 4 stitches.

I-Cord Round: Knit across; without turning your work, slip the row to the other end of the needle; pull the yarn across the back to begin the next round. Repeat the I-cord round for 24 rounds or desired length.

*

RECEPTACLE (FLOWER FOUNDATION)

Round 1: Change to B and knit around.

Round 2: Kfb around—8 stitches. Divide the stitches between 2 needles.

Round 3: Kfb around—16 stitches. Divide the stitches among 4 needles.

Round 4: Join a strand of E; with B and E held together, *kfb, k1, M1, k1, kfb; repeat from * around—28 stitches.

Put the stitches on separate holders as follows: *3 stitches on a holder held to the outside (for a petal), 1 stitch on a different-colored holder held to the center (for the flower center), 3 stitches on a holder the same color as the 1st holder, held to the outside; repeat from * 3 more times. There will be 8 petal holders with 3 stitches each and 1 flower center holder with 4 stitches.

*

PISTIL

Transfer the 4 flower center stitches to a single double-pointed needle.

Holding the live strand of B and E together, work as an I-cord for 3 rounds. Cut the yarns, leaving a long tail. Using a tapestry needle, draw the yarn through the remaining 4 stitches and pull tight. Weave the end into the center and secure.

*

1ST PETAL

Transfer 1 set of 3 stitches to a needle.

Row 1 (RS): With the stem side of the flower facing down and the center of the flower facing up toward you, join a long strand of C; k3.

Row 2 (WS): P1 with C, join a strand of D and p1; join a new long strand of C and p1—3 stitches.

Row 3: C: kfb; D: k1; C: kfb—5 stitches.

Row 4: Purl in established color pattern.

Row 5: C: k1, M1-R, k1; D: kfbf; C: k1, M1-L, k1—9 stitches.

Row 6: C: p3; D: k1, p1, k1; C: p3.

Row 7: C: k1, M1-R, k2; D: p1, kfb, p1; C: k2, M1-L, k1—12 stitches.

Row 8: C: p4; D: k1, p2, k1; C: p4—12 stitches.

Row 9: C: k1, M1-R, k3; D: p1, k2, p1; C: k3, M1-L, k1—14 stitches.

Row 10: C: p5; D: k1, p2, k1; C: p5.

Row 11: C: k5; D: p1, k2, p1; C: k5.

Row 12: Repeat row 10.

Row 13 (short row): Work 12 stitches in the established color and stitch pattern, W&T.

Row 14 (short row): Work 10 stitches in the established color and stitch pattern, W&T.

Rows 15–24: Work the established color and stitch pattern across all stitches.

Row 25: C: k1, ssk, k2; D: p1, k2, p1; C: k2, k2tog, k1— 12 stitches.

Row 26: C: p4; D: k1, p2tog, k1; C: p4—11 stitches.

Row 27: C: k1, ssk, k1; D: p1, k1, p1; C: k1, k2tog, k1—9 stitches.

Row 28: C: p1, p2tog; D: k1, p1, k1; C: ssp, p1—7 stitches.

Row 29: C: k2; D: sk2p; C: k2—5 stitches.

Row 30: C: p2; D: p1; C: p2—5 stitches.

Row 31: C: k2; D: k1; C: k2—5 stitches.

Row 32: C: p2tog; D: p1; C: ssp—3 stitches.

Row 33: C: sk2p—1 stitch.

Cut the yarn and draw the end through the remaining stitch to fasten off.

*

2ND–8TH PETALS

Work as for the 1st petal.

Weave in ends at the apex and base of each petal.

*

FINISHING

Stamens: Cut 12 strands (or sufficient strands to encircle the pistil) of B 3" (7.5cm) long, adjusting the strand length for smaller- or larger-gauge flowers. For instructions on making stamens refer to page 30. Trim the strands to approximately ½" (13mm) or appropriately scaled length.

Creeping
Phlox

Phlox subulata

DIFFICULTY LEVEL 〇〇〇〇

REQUIRED YARN COLORS

Green (A) and white, pink, or purple (B)
Lighter-gauge yarn for embroidery in
orange (C) and raspberry (D) (optional)

SAMPLE

Finished Measurements
Flower head diameter: 3" (7.5cm)
Stem length: 2" (5cm)

Yarns Used
Stonehedge Fiber Mill *Shepherd's Wool*
(worsted weight) Lime (A), Pink (B),
and (fingering weight) Orange (C)
and Raspberry (D)

PEDUNCLE
(MAIN STEM)

With A, cast on 2 stitches.

I-Cord Round: Knit across; without turning your work, slip the row to the other end of the needle; pull the yarn across the back to begin the next round.

Repeat the I-cord round for 12 rounds or desired length.

✳

RECEPTACLE
(FLOWER FOUNDATION)

Round 1: [Kfb] twice—4 stitches.
Round 2: Knit around.
Round 3: K2, M1, k2—5 stitches.
Divide the stitches between 2 needles.
Rounds 4 and 5: Knit around.
Round 6: Join a strand of B; with A and B held together, knit around.
Transfer the 5 A stitches to holders to the outside for the sepal leaves, keeping the 5 B stitches on the needles to continue working.
Rounds 7 and 8: With B, knit around.
Round 9: Purl around; W&T.
Round 10: Going in the opposite direction, kfb in each stitch—10 stitches.
Round 11: Knit around. Cut the yarn and weave in the ends.
Transfer 8 stitches to 4 holders (2 stitches on each); keep 2 stitches on a needle to work the 1st petal.

1ST PETAL

Position the flower so that the peduncle and petal underside are facing away and the flower center is facing you.
Row 1 (RS): Join a new strand of B; k1, M1, k1—3 stitches.
Row 2: P3.
Row 3: K1, kfb, k1—4 stitches.
Row 4: P4.
Row 5: K2, M1, k2—5 stitches.
Rows 6–8: Work in stockinette stitch.
Row 9: K2, bind off 1, k2.
Row 10: *P2, turn, k2tog, cut the yarn and draw the end through the remaining stitch; join a new strand and repeat from * once more on the remaining 2 stitches.
Weave in the ends along the underside edge base and tips of the petals so that the petal tips appear blunt and rounded.

✳

2ND–5TH PETALS

Transfer the 2 stitches to the left of the petal just completed to a needle. Join a new strand of B and work as for the 1st petal.

✳

SEPAL LEAVES

Transfer the 5 A stitches to 2 needles. Join a new strand of A.
Bind-off Row: Using the backwards-loop cast-on method, *cast on 3 stitches and bind off 4; slip the remaining stitch from the right-hand onto the left-hand needle and repeat from * until all 5 stitches have been bound off.

Cut the yarn and weave in the end so that the first and last sepal leaves sit snugly next to each other to complete the round of sepal leaves.

✳

EMBROIDERY

With a darning needle and C, use small straight stitches in the flower center to replicate the small orange pistil and stamens (see photo).
With D, make 2 dots of raspberry at the base of each petal using straight stitch or French knots that are invisible on the petal underside (see photo).

Crocus
Crocus chrysanthus

DIFFICULTY LEVEL ⬦⬦⬦⬦

REQUIRED YARN COLORS

Green (A) and purple (B), lighter-gauge yarn in white (C), and bright yellow (D)

SAMPLE

Finished Measurements
Flower head diameter (with petals extended to the side): 5" (12.5cm)
Stem length: 5" (12.5cm)

Yarns Used
Stonehedge Fiber Mill *Shepherd's Wool* (worsted weight) Lime Green (A) and Lilac (B) and (fingering weight) White (C) and Sun Yellow (D)

PATTERN NOTES

- Requires needles approximately 5 sizes smaller for the pistil and stamen.
- When working across short rows, there is no need to hide the wraps.

INSTRUCTIONS

PEDUNCLE (MAIN STEM)

With A, cast on 2 stitches.
I-Cord Round: Knit across; without turning your work, slip the row to the other end of the needle; pull the yarn across the back to begin the next round.
Repeat the I-cord round for 36 rounds.

RECEPTACLE (FLOWER FOUNDATION)

Round 1: Change to B and knit. Cut A and tie the ends of A and B in a square knot; weave in the strand of A down the peduncle and weave in the strand of B on a petal underside edge once the petals are complete.
Round 2: Kfbf in each stitch—6 stitches.
Divide the stitches between 2 needles.
Round 3: With a strand of B and a strand of C held together, knit around.
Slip all 6 B stitches onto needles held to the outside for petals. Slip the C stitches onto holders as follows: Slip the 1st, 3rd, and 5th stitches onto a holder held to the center for the pistil. Slip the remaining 3 stitches onto holders held between the B stitches and center C stitches for the stamens. Cut C and tie the 2 ends together in a square knot to secure. Weave in the ends inside the pistil once it has been completed.
Round 4: With B, kfb around—12 stitches.
Round 5: Knit around.

✳

1ST PETAL

Transfer all but the last 2 stitches of the round to 5 holders (2 stitches on each holder) for the last 5 petals. Reposition the flower so that the flower center is facing you and the peduncle is facing away.
Row 1 (RS—the inside of the flower and the right side of the petal are now facing you): K1, M1, k1—3

stitches.
Row 2: P3.
Row 3: K1, M1-R, k1, M1-L, k1—5 stitches.
Row 4: P5.
Row 5: K1, M1-R, k3, M1-L, k1—7 stitches.
Row 6 (short row): P5, W&T.
Row 7 (short row): K3, W&T.
Row 8: P5.
Row 9: K7.
Row 10: P7.
Row 11 (short row): K5, W&T.
Row 12 (short row): P3, W&T.
Row 13: K5.
Row 14: P7.
Row 15: K7.
Row 16 (short row): P5, W&T.
Row 17 (short row): K3, W&T.
Row 18: P5.
Row 19: Ssk, k3, k2tog—5 stitches.
Row 20: P2tog, p1, ssp—3 stitches.
Row 21: Sk2p—1 stitch.
Cut the yarn and pull the tail through the remaining stitch to fasten off. Weave in the end along the petal underside edge so that the tip of the petal looks rounded.

✳

2ND–6TH PETALS

Transfer the 2 stitches to the left of the petal just completed to a needle. Join a new strand of B and work as for the 1st petal.

✳

PISTIL

Style: With D and the smaller needles, work the 3 center C stitches as an I-cord for 12 rounds.

Stigma: Kfb in each stitch—6 stitches. Turn the work and kfb in each stitch—12 stitches. Bind off the stitches using the sewn bind-off (page 23). The resulting stigma looks like a little battle axe (but you're not finished with it yet!); fold it in 3 so that it looks more like a little ruffle and then tack it in place using the strand still attached to the needle. Weave the ends into the center of the pistil.

*

STAMENS

Transfer the 3 C stitches from holders to 2 smaller needles. Join a new strand of C, and working in the round (around the pistil—this is a bit awkward, but not difficult), [kfb] 3 times—6 stitches. Leave the last 2 stitches worked on a needle and transfer the remaining 4 stitches to holders in groups of 2 for the filaments.

1st filament: Knit the 2 stitches as an I-cord for 7 rounds.

Next round: Change to D and k2tog—1 stitch.

Anther: Using the backwards-loop cast-on method, cast on 5 stitches. Bind off the stitches. Cut the yarn. Weave in the end so as to tack the anther against the filament so that the anther aligns itself vertically with its filament and faces away from the pistil.

2nd and 3rd filaments: Transfer the 2 stitches to the left of the filament just completed to a smaller needle. Join a

new strand of D and work as for the 1st filament and anther.

*

FINISHING

Once all the filaments and anthers are complete, you may find it necessary to use a strand of C to tack the

base of the filaments together so that they stand up smartly.

Arrange the crocus petals so that every other petal sits slightly inside its 3 alternate counterparts. Tack as necessary to maintain this petal placement.

For best results, wire the petals in the above configuration.

Cyclamen

Cyclamen hederifolium

REQUIRED YARN COLORS

Dark red or brown (A), true red (B), hot pink (C), and medium pink (D)

SAMPLE

Finished Measurements
Flower head diameter (with petals extended to the side): 6" (15cm); (with petals standing up): 1" (2.5cm)
Stem length: 6" (15cm)

Yarns Used
Stonehedge Fiber Mill *Shepherd's Wool* (worsted weight) Midnight Lake (A), Christmas Red (B), Hot Pink (C), and Zinnia Pink (D)

INSTRUCTIONS

PEDUNCLE
(MAIN STEM)

With A, cast on 2 stitches.
I-Cord Round: Knit across; without turning your work, slip the row to the other end of the needle; pull the yarn across the back to begin the next round.
Repeat the I-cord round for 36 rounds or desired length.

*

RECEPTACLE
(FLOWER FOUNDATION)

Round 1: Kfb in each stitch—4 stitches.
Round 2: Knit around.
Round 3: Kfb in each stitch—8 stitches.

Divide stitches between 2 needles.
Round 4: Knit around.
Round 5: [K2, M1, k2] twice—10 stitches.
Rounds 6 and 7: Knit around.
Round 8: Change to B and knit.
Rounds 9 and 10: Purl around.
Transfer the first 8 stitches to 4 holders (2 stitches on each), keeping the last 2 stitches on a needle for the 1st petal. Use the live strand of B to work the 1st petal.

*

1ST PETAL

Position the flower so that the flower center is facing you.
Row 1 (RS): With B, [kfb] twice —4 stitches.
Row 2: P4.
Row 3: K1, LI-R, k2, LI-L, k1—6 stitches.
Row 4: P6.
For 1-color petals, continue with B for row 5; for color-graded petals, change to C for row 5.
Row 5: K1, LI-R, k4, LI-L, k1—8 stitches.
Row 6: P8.
For 1-color petals, continue with B for row 7; for color-graded petals, change to D for row 7.
Row 7: K1, LI-R, k6, LI-L, k1—10 stitches.
Rows 8–16: Work in stockinette stitch.
Row 17: K1, ssk, knit to the last 3 stitches, k2tog, k1 —8 stitches.
Row 18: P8.
Row 19: Repeat row 17—6 stitches.
Row 20: P6.
Row 21: Ssk, k2, k2tog—4 stitches.

Row 22: P4.
Row 23: Ssk, k2tog and bind off at the same time.
Cut the yarn. Weave in the ends at the base and the apex of the petal along the underside edges. For color-graded petals, tie the ends in square knots (right over left, left over right) and weave in the ends vertically along same-color stitches.

*

2ND–5TH PETALS

Transfer the 2 stitches to the left of the petal just completed to a needle.
Join a new strand of B and work as for the 1st petal.

*

FINISHING

For both felted and unfelted versions of the flower, tack the petals to the flower receptacle to help hold the cyclamen shape.
Thread the stem through the petals at their base so that the flower "looks" down and the stem is gracefully curved.

Daffodil

Narcissus pseudo-narcissus

REQUIRED YARN COLORS

Green (A), pale yellow (B), white (C),
medium yellow (D), and (optional)
orange or beaded yellow (E)

SAMPLE

Finished Measurements
Flower head diameter: 6" (15cm)
Stem length: 10" (25.5cm)

Yarns Used
Flower 1 (previous page, far right):
Stonehedge Fiber Mill *Shepherd's Wool*
(worsted weight) Lime Green (A),
Spring Chick (B, C, and D), and Tilli
Tomas *Flurries* Saffron (E)
Flower 2 (previous page, center):
Stonehedge Fiber Mill *Shepherd's Wool*
(worsted weight) Lime Green (A),
Spring Chick (B), White (C), Sun
Yellow (D), and Tilli Tomas *Flurries*
Saffron (E)
Flower 3 (previous page, lightly felted
flower at bottom left): Stonehedge
Fiber Mill *Shepherd's Wool* (worsted
weight) Lime Green (A), Spring Chick
(B), Tilli Tomas *Flurries* Saffron (C),
and Creamsicle (D)
Flower 4 (previous page, felted flower
at far left): Stonehedge Fiber Mill
Shepherd's Wool (worsted weight) Lime
Green (A), Spring Chick (B), White
(C), and Sun Yellow (D)
Flower 5 (previous page, center top):
Stonehedge Fiber Mill *Shepherd's Wool*
(worsted weight) Lime Green (A),
Spring Chick (B), White (C), Sun
Yellow (D), and Creamsicle (E)

INSTRUCTIONS

PEDUNCLE (MAIN STEM)

With A, cast on 3 stitches.

I-Cord Round: Knit across; without
turning your work, slip the row to the
other end of the needle; pull the yarn
across the back to begin the next
round.

Repeat the I-cord round for 60 rounds
or desired length.

✳

RECEPTACLE
(FLOWER FOUNDATION)
& SETUP FOR PISTIL

Round 1: Kfb in each stitch—6
stitches.
Divide the stitches between 2 needles.
Rounds 2–5: Knit around.
Round 6: [K1, k2tog] twice—4
stitches.
Round 7: Knit around.
Round 8: K1, M1-R, k2, M1-L, k1—6
stitches.
Round 9: Join a strand of B; with A
and B held together, knit around.
Transfer the 6 A stitches to 2 parallel needles or 2 holders held to the
outside. Transfer the 6 B stitches to a
single needle, held to center, to work
the pistil as follows.

✳

PISTIL

Round 1: K2tog around—3 stitches.
Round 2: Ssk, k1—2 stitches.
Rounds 3–9: Knit around. Cut yarn
and draw tail through the remaining
2 stitches. Weave in the end.

RECEPTACLE
(CONTINUED)

Return to the 6 A stitches on 2 holders or needles (if they're on holders,
transfer them to 2 parallel needles).
Round 10: With the live strand of A,
[k1, kfb] 3 times—9 stitches.
Round 11: Kfb in each stitch—18
stitches. Cut A.
Round 12: Change to C and knit
around. Tie the A and B ends together
and weave A down the stem center to
secure.
Round 13: With C, kfb around—36
stitches. Transfer every other stitch to
3 holders held to the center for the
center flute—18 stitches. At the same
time, transfer the remaining stitches to
2 parallel needles held to the outside.
Now that this has been accomplished,
keep the first 3 outside stitches of the
round on a needle to make the 1st
petal; move the remaining 15 outside
stitches to 5 holders (3 stitches on
each) held to the outside for the last
5 petals; move the remaining 18 C
stitches to 3 holders (6 stitches each)
held to the center for the center flute.

✳

1ST PETAL

Row 1 (WS): Position the flower so
that the flower center is facing away
from you and the peduncle is facing
down and is between you and the
petal you are working: P3 with C.
Row 2 (RS): The right side of the petals are facing you when the flower
center is facing you: K1, M1-R, k1,
M1-L, k1—5 stitches.
Row 3: P5.

Row 4: K1, M1-R, kfb, k1, kfb, M1-L, k1—9 stitches.

Row 5: P9.

Row 6: K1, M1-R, k7, M1-L, k1—11 stitches.

Row 7: P11.

Row 8: K1, M1-R, k9, M1-L, k1—13 stitches.

Row 9: P13.

Row 10: K1, ssk, knit to last 3 stitches, k2tog, k1—11 stitches.

Row 11: P11.

Row 12: Repeat row 10—9 stitches.

Row 13: P9.

Row 14: Repeat row 10—7 stitches.

Row 15: P7.

Row 16: Repeat row 10—5 stitches.

Row 17: P5.

Row 18: Ssk, k1, k2tog—3 stitches.

Row 19: S1, ssp, psso—1 stitch.

Cut the yarn and draw the tail through the remaining stitch to fasten off.

Weave in the end on the underside edge of the petal.

*

2ND–6TH PETALS

Transfer the set of 3 stitches to the left of the petal just completed to a needle. Join a new strand of C and complete as for the 1st petal, weaving in the ends at the base and apex of each petal along petal underside edges.

CENTER FLUTE

Transfer the 18 C stitches to 3 double-pointed needles. Mark the beginning of the round and join.

Round 1: If the desired color for the flute is different than the petals, change to D and [k2, p1] 6 times.

Rounds 2–8: Work in the established pattern around.

Note: For a flower with a short flute, stop after round 5 and proceed to round 13.

Round 9: K1, [M1, work 4 stitches in the established pattern] 4 times, p1—22 stitches.

Round 10: Work in the established pattern, knitting all new stitches from round 9.

Note: For a medium-short flute, stop here and proceed to round 13.

Rounds 11–14: Work in the established pattern.

Note: For a flower with a longer flute, continue in pattern for 2 more rounds or desired length, then proceed to the bind-off round.

Bind-off Round: If desired, change to E and, using a cable cast-on method, *cast on 2 stitches, then bind off 3 stitches; move the remaining stitch from the right-hand needle onto the left-hand needle; cast on 1 stitch, then bind off 3 stitches; slip the remaining stitch from the right-hand needle onto the left-hand needle; repeat from * until all stitches are bound off. Weave in the end so that the first and last stitch to be bound off sit snugly next to each other.

FINISHING

For best results, wire the stems and petals.

Dahlia

Dahlia

DIFFICULTY LEVEL ⬠⬠⬠⬠

REQUIRED YARN COLORS
Green (A), dark red/wine or desired
color (B), and yellow-green (C)

SAMPLE
Finished Measurements
Flower head diameter: 4" (10cm)
Stem length: 6" (15cm)

Yarns Used
Stonehedge Fiber Mill *Shepherd's Wool*
(worsted weight) Lime (A), Garnet
(B), and Spring Green (C)

PEDUNCLE (MAIN STEM)

With A, cast on 3 stitches.

I-Cord Round: Knit across; without turning your work, slip the row to the other end of the needle; pull the yarn across the back to begin the next round.

Repeat the I-cord round for 36 rounds or desired length.

✳

RECEPTACLE (FLOWER FOUNDATION)

Round 1: Kfb, k1, kfb—5 stitches.

Round 2: Knit around.

Round 3: Join a strand of C; with A and C held together, knit around. *Do not cut the yarns.*

Round 4: Slip the 5 A stitches onto 2 needles held to the outside to continue the receptacle (below); transfer the 5 C stitches to a single needle held to the center for the pistil.

✳

PISTIL

Work pistil stitches as an I-cord:

Rounds 1 and 2: With C, knit around—5 stitches.

Cut the yarn and draw the tail through the 5 stitches on the needle, pulling tight. Weave in the end down the center of the flower pistil and peduncle so that the strand of C does not show.

RECEPTACLE (CONTINUED)

Round 5: Join a strand of B; with A and B held together, knit around. *Do not cut the yarns.*

Round 6: Transfer the 5 B stitches to holders held to the center for the interior petals, keeping the 5 A stitches on the 2 parallel working needles.

Round 7: With A, kfb in each stitch—10 stitches.

Round 8: Knit around.

Round 9: Join a strand of B; with A and B held together, knit around. *Do not cut the yarns.*

Keep the first 2 A stitches worked during round 9 on a needle; transfer the remaining 8 A stitches to 2 holders held to the outside for the sepal leaves; transfer the 10 B stitches to holders held between the A stitches and the center B stitches.

✳

1ST SEPAL LEAF

Position the flower so that the peduncle is facing toward you and the center is facing away—this orients the sepal leaves so that the wrong side is facing the petal undersides.

Row 1 (RS): K1, M1, k1—3 stitches.

Rows 2–4: Work in stockinette stitch.

Row 5: Sk2p—1 stitch.

Weave in the ends along the wrong-side edge of the sepal.

✳

2ND–5TH SEPAL LEAVES

Transfer the 2 stitches to the left of the petal just completed to a needle.

Join a new strand of A and work as for 1st sepal.

✳

INTERIOR PETALS

Transfer the 5 B stitches held in the center to 2 needles.

Row 1 (RS): Using the live strand of B, kfb in each stitch, turn—10 stitches.

Bind-off Row: Using the backwards-loop cast-on method, *cast on 7 stitches, then bind off 8 stitches; slip the remaining stitch from the right- to the left-hand needle and repeat from * until all 10 stitches have been bound off.

Cut the yarn and weave in the end.

✳

EXTERIOR PETALS

Divide the 10 B stitches held at center between 2 or more needles.

Join a new strand of B and work in rows, adding more double-pointed needles when it is comfortable to do so.

Row 1 (WS): P10.

Row 2 (RS): Kfb in each stitch—20 stitches.

Row 3: Kfbf in each stitch—60 stitches.

Bind-off Row: Using the backwards-loop cast-on method, *cast on 12 stitches, then bind off 13 stitches; slip the remaining stitch from the right- to the left-hand needle; repeat from * until all 60 stitches are bound off. Cut the yarn, leaving a long tail.

Use the tail to join the first petal to the last at the base of the receptacle. Weave in the ends.

Dogwood
Cornus florida

DIFFICULTY LEVEL ✎✎✎✎

REQUIRED YARN COLORS
Gray (A), white (B), pale pink (C), pink (D), medium pink (E), and medium green (F)

SAMPLE
Finished Measurements
Flower head diameter: 4" (10cm)
Stem length: 1" (2.5cm)

Yarns Used
Stonehedge Fiber Mill *Shepherd's Wool* (worsted weight) Milk Chocolate (A), White (B), Baby Pink (C), Pink (D), Zinnia Pink (E), and Lime Green (F)

PATTERN NOTE
When working across short rows, there is no need to hide the wraps.

INSTRUCTIONS

PEDUNCLE (MAIN STEM)
With A, cast on 2 stitches.
I-Cord Round: Knit across; without turning your work, slip the row to the other end of the needle; pull the yarn across the back to begin the next round. Repeat the I-cord round for 6 rounds or desired length.

*

RECEPTACLE (FLOWER FOUNDATION)
Note: Every round of the flower center is worked as for an I-cord.

Round 1: Change to B; k1, M1, k1—3 stitches.
Round 2: Knit around.
Round 3: K1, kfb, k1—4 stitches.
Round 4: Knit around.
Round 5: K1, M1, k2, M1, k1—6 stitches.
Divide the stitches between 2 needles.
Round 6: Kfb in each stitch—12 stitches.
Round 7: Knit around.

*

1ST SEPAL LEAF
For the sake of accuracy, I will refer to the dogwood "petals" as sepal leaves. Transfer the first 9 stitches to 3 holders (3 stitches on each) and turn to work the 1st sepal leaf on the remaining 3 stitches.

Row 1 (WS): Position the flower so that the peduncle is facing up and the flower center is facing away from you; change to C, p3.
Row 2 (RS): K1, M1-R, k1, M1-L, k1—5 stitches.
Row 3: Purl.
Row 4: Change to D; k1, M1-R, k3, M1-L, k1—7 stitches.
Row 5 (short row): P2, W&T.
Row 6: K2.
Row 7: P7.
Row 8 (short row): K2, W&T.
Row 9: P2.
Row 10: Change to E; k1, M1-R, k5, M1-L, k1—9 stitches.
Row 11 (short row): P6, W&T.
Row 12 (short row): K3, W&T.
Row 13: P6.
Row 14: K1, M1-R, k7, M1-L, k1—11 stitches.

Row 15 (short row): P3, W&T.
Row 16: K3.
Row 17: P11.
Row 18 (short row): K3, W&T.
Row 19: P3.
Row 20: K11.
Row 21: P11.
Row 22: K2, ssk, k3, k2tog, k2—9 stitches.
Row 23: Purl.
Row 24: K2, ssk, k1, k2tog, k2—7 stitches.
Row 25: P1, p2tog, p1, ssp, p1—5 stitches.
Row 26: Change to A; ssk, k1, k2tog and *at the same time* bind off.
Tie the tails of the color changes together and weave in all ends on the sepal leaf underside edges.

*

2ND–4TH SEPAL LEAVES
Transfer the 3 stitches to the left of the petal just completed to a needle. Complete as for the 1st sepal.

*

FINISHING
To prepare dogwoods for felting, weave in the tail at the apex of each sepal. Where a new color was joined, tie ends in a square knot or wrap around each other and weave in on petal underside edges or horizontally across like-color fields.
To replicate the tiny dogwood flower buds in the center of the sepal leaves, use F and a sharp needle to put a few French knots in the center of the flower *before felting.*

English
Bluebell

Hyacinthoides non-scripta

DIFFICULTY LEVEL 𝒫 ⵔ ⵔ ⵔ

REQUIRED YARN COLORS

Green (A), blue (B), and white (C)

SAMPLE

Finished Measurements

Flower head diameter: 1½" (4cm)
Stem length: 12" (30.5cm) from base
to final flower

Yarns Used

Stonehedge Fiber Mill *Shepherd's Wool*
(worsted weight) Lime (A) and Misty
Blue (B)

INSTRUCTIONS

PEDUNCLE (MAIN STEM)

With A, cast on 4 stitches.

I-Cord Round: Knit across; without
turning your work, slip the row to the
other end of the needle; pull the yarn
across the back to begin the next
round.

Repeat the I-cord round for 18 rounds
or desired length.

Next round: K1, ssk, k1—3 stitches.

Work 12 more I-cord rounds.

Next round: K1, k2tog—2 stitches.

Work 12 more I-cord rounds.

SETUP FOR PEDICELS (BRANCHING STEMS)

*Setup round for 1st pedicel: [Kfb]
twice—4 stitches.

Next round: K2, put the next 2
stitches on a holder unworked—2
stitches remain.

Work 7 I-cord rounds.

Repeat from * 4 times more—5 sets of
pedicel stitches on holders.

Work 3 more I-cord rounds.

*

MAIN FLOWER

Rounds 1–7: Change to B; work 7
I-cord rounds.

Round 8: Kfbf in each stitch—6
stitches. Divide the stitches between 2
needles.

Rounds 9–13: Knit in the round.

Bind-off round: Using the backwards-loop cast-on method, *cast on
5 stitches; bind off 6 stitches; slip the
remaining stitch from the right-hand
needle onto the left-hand needle;
repeat from * until all stitches are
bound off.

Attach the first petal to the last as you
weave in ends.

BRANCHING FLOWERS (MAKE 5)

For each branching flower, transfer a
set of the pedicel stitches to a needle
and work as for the Main Flower.

*

FINISHING

Wire the peduncle and pedicels (after
felting), allowing blossoms to dangle
at the end of each pedicel.

Forget-Me-Not

Brunnera macrophylia

DIFFICULTY LEVEL 🍃 🍃 🍃

REQUIRED YARN COLORS

Green (A), yellow or white (B), and medium blue (C)

SAMPLE

Finished Measurements

Flower head diameter: 4" (10cm)

Yarns Used

Stonehedge Fiber Mill *Shepherd's Wool* (worsted weight) White (A) and Baby Blue (1st flower) or Misty Blue (B)

INSTRUCTIONS

PEDUNCLE (MAIN STEM)

With A, cast on 2 stitches.

I-Cord Round: Knit across; without turning your work, slip the row to the other end of the needle; pull the yarn across the back to begin the next round.

Repeat the I-cord round for 6 rounds or the desired length.

RECEPTACLE (FLOWER FOUNDATION)

Round 1: Kfb in each stitch—4 stitches.

Round 2: Change to B; k2, M1, k2—5 stitches.

Round 3: Kfb in each stitch—10 stitches. Divide the stitches between 2 double-pointed needles.

Round 4: Purl around.

*

1ST PETAL

Keep the first 2 stitches of the round on the needle for the 1st petal; put the remaining 8 stitches on 4 holders (2 stitches each) for the last 4 petals. Position the flower so that the flower center is facing you.

Row 1 (RS): K1, M1, k1—3 stitches.

Row 2 (WS): P3.

Row 3: Kfb in each stitch—6 stitches.

Row 4: Purl.

Row 5: K1, LI-R, k4, LI-L, k1—8 stitches.

Rows 6–12: Work in stockinette stitch.

Row 13: Ssk, k4, k2tog—6 stitches.

Row 14: Purl.

Row 15: Ssk, k2, k2tog—4 stitches.

Bind off the remaining 4 stitches purlwise.

Cut the yarn and weave in ends at the apex and base of each petal.

2ND–5TH PETALS

Transfer the 2 stitches to the left of the petal just completed to a needle. Join a new strand of B and work as for 1st petal.

*

FINISHING

Weave the tails at the base of each petal into the petal underside edges after first taking an invisible stitch in the flower center in order to strengthen the intersection of flower petal and center.

To block flowers, first felt them according to the general felting instructions (page 160). Place flowers on a smooth surface with the right side facing you. Smooth out each petal between your fingers, making each petal cup toward you by placing your thumb in the center of the petal and your fingers on the underside opposite your thumb. You may want to let the flowers dry in shallow bowls or muffin tins to give them a nice curved shape.

Fuchsia

Fuchsia aintree

DIFFICULTY LEVEL 🖊🖊🖊🖊

REQUIRED YARN COLORS
Green (A), white (B), and pale or medium pink (C)

SAMPLE
Finished Measurements
Flower height from receptacle to flower tips: 5" (12.5cm)
Stem length: 2" (5cm)

Yarns Used
Stonehedge Fiber Mill *Shepherd's Wool* (worsted weight) Lime Green (A), White (B), and Zinnia Pink (C)

INSTRUCTIONS

PEDUNCLE (MAIN STEM)
With A, cast on 2 stitches.
I-Cord Round: Knit across; without turning your work, slip the row to the other end of the needle; pull the yarn across the back to begin the next round.
Repeat the I-cord round for 18 rounds or desired length.

*For More Than
One Flower on One Stem*

For a profusion of flowers dripping off 1 stem, kfb in each stitch—4 stitches. Slip the first 2 stitches onto a holder; keep the second 2 stitches on the needle and continue to work as an I-cord.
Once the peduncle is complete, return to the 2 stitches on a holder, join a strand of A and work as an I-cord for the desired length before following

the instructions for the receptacle and then exterior and interior petals.

＊

RECEPTACLE (FLOWER FOUNDATION)
Round 1: Kfb in each stitch—4 stitches.
Round 2: Knit around.
Round 3: K1, M1, k2, M1, k1—6 stitches.
Round 4: Knit.
Round 5: Change to B and k2tog around—3 stitches.
Round 6: Knit around.
Round 7: Kfb in each stitch—6 stitches.
Round 8: [K1, kfb, k1] twice—8 stitches.
Divide the stitches between 2 needles.
Rounds 9 and 10: Knit around.
Round 11: K2, k2tog, k2, k2tog—6 stitches.
Round 12: Kfb in each stitch—12 stitches.
Divide the stitches among 4 needles.
Round 13: Knit around.
Round 14: Kfb in each stitch—24 stitches.
Starting at the beginning of the round, *[transfer the 1st stitch to a holder held to the center, transfer the next stitch to a different-colored holder held to the outside] 3 times, ending with 3 stitches on 1 holder in the center for an interior petal and 3 stitches on another holder held to the outside for an exterior petal. Repeat from * 3 more times using new holders for each set of petal stitches—12 stitches on 4 holders in the center and

12 stitches on 4 holders held to the outside. Cut all strands of yarn and tie ends of like strands together in square knots and weave in the ends.

＊

1ST EXTERIOR PETAL
Transfer the first 3 exterior petal stitches to a needle.
Position the piece so that the peduncle and receptacle are facing you and the flower center is facing away from you.
Row 1 (RS): Join a new strand of B, kfb, k1, kfb—5 stitches.
Row 2: P5.
Row 3: K1, M1-R, k3, M1-L, k1—7 stitches.
Rows 4 and 6: P3, k1, p3.
Row 5: K3, p1, k3.
Row 7: K1, M1-R, k2, p1, k2, M1-L, k1—9 stitches.
Row 8: P4, k1, p4.
Row 9: K4, p1, k4.
Rows 10–16: Work stitches as they appear (RS: K4, p1, k4; WS: P4, k1, p4).
Row 17: K1, ssk, k1, p1, k1, k2tog, k1—7 stitches.
Row 18: P3, k1, p3.
Row 19: K1, ssk, p1, k2tog, k1—5 stitches.
Row 20: P2, k1, p2.
Row 21: K1, sk2p, k1—3 stitches.
Row 22: P3.
Row 23: Sk2p—1 stitch.
Cut the yarn and pull the end through the remaining stitch. Weave in the end along the petal underside edge. Work remaining exterior petals as for the 1st.

1ST INTERIOR PETAL

Transfer a set of 3 interior petal stitches to a needle.

Position the flower so that the center is facing you and the peduncle is facing away. With the 1st row of the petal, you establish the petal underside (WS) as facing inward toward the flower.

Row 1 (WS): Join a strand of C and p3.

Row 2 (RS): Kfb in each stitch—6 stitches.

Row 3: P6.

Row 4: K1, M1-R, knit to last stitch, M1-L, k1—8 stitches.

Row 5: P8.

Row 6: Repeat row 4—10 stitches.

Rows 7–11: Work in stockinette stitch.

Row 12: K1, ssk, k4, k2tog, k1—8 stitches.

Row 13: P8.

Row 14: K1, ssk, k2, k2tog, k1—6 stitches.

Row 15: P2tog, p2, ssp and *at the same time* bind off the stitches.

Cut the yarn and weave in the end along the wrong side of the petal edge.

*

2ND–4TH INTERIOR PETALS

Transfer the 3 stitches to the left of the petal just completed to a needle. Join a new strand of C and work as for the 1st petal.

PISTIL

To make the pistil, cut a 15" (38cm) strand of B, or the necessary strand length for the gauge flower you are working. Thread 1 end on a darning needle. Turn the flower upside down and turn back the interior petals to reveal the flower underside center. Place the tip of the needle through the center surface as if sewing and pull one end through the flower center; then take the strand off the needle and tie the tail to itself, using a square knot. Secure the short end by weaving it in. For worsted-weight flowers, the center strand should measure no less than 13" (33cm) at this point or about 3 times the height of the blossom. If felting, trim after felting: The strands shrink a lot. If not felting, trim so that the pistil is quite visible below the interior and exterior petals. Refer to the sample photo or to pictures of actual fuchsia flowers to guide your efforts.

*

STAMENS

To make the 6 filaments, cut three 12" (30cm) strands of B, or the appropriately scaled strand length for the gauge flower you are making. Refer to page 30 for instructions on making stamens. Once stamens are complete, tie a little knot at the end of each of the 6 filaments. If felting, trim away any fringy bits created by the felting process and sew 1 silver, white, or pale pink tiny seed bead to each knot to suggest the anther. If not felting, trim so that anthers are visible below the interior petals. To ensure that the knots do not come untied, dot them with fabric glue to secure.

*

FINISHING

Weave in all remaining ends along the petal underside edges, strengthening the joints of the petals as you do so. Use a darning needle and a strand of C to tack the interior petals to one another so that the right side of each petal overlaps its neighbor in such a way that the bell shape of the interior petals is achieved.

You may also find it necessary to tack the exterior petals to the interior ones about halfway down the exterior petal. You can coax the lower part of the petal to curl upward either by pressing your thumb into the top side with your first and middle fingers, and massaging the inside of the petal upward, or by simply wiring the exterior petals (page 32) so that the curl stays all by itself.

Gardenia

Gardenia grandiflora

DIFFICULTY LEVEL ◊◊◊◊

REQUIRED YARN COLORS
Brown (A), green (B), and white (C)

SAMPLE
Finished Measurements
Flower head diameter: 6" (15cm)
Stem length: 4" (10cm)

Yarns Used
Universal Yarn *Deluxe Worsted*
Excalibur #6347 (A), Greenery
#61633 (B), and White #12257 (C)

PATTERN NOTE
When using white yarns with the
intention of felting, please swatch first
to determine how readily a particular
white will felt.

PEDUNCLE (MAIN STEM)

With A, cast on 3 stitches.

I-Cord Round: Knit across; without turning your work, slip the row to the other end of the needle; pull the yarn across the back to begin the next round.

Repeat the I-cord round for 12 rounds.

✳

RECEPTACLE (FLOWER FOUNDATION)

Round 1: K1, M1, k1, M1, k1—5 stitches.

Round 2: Join a strand of B and a strand of C; with B and C held together, knit around. Cut A, tie in a square knot with B, and weave in the end down the center of the peduncle. Transfer the C stitches to a holder held to the center—these stitches will be worked as small center petals later. Cut C and weave in the ends. Transfer the B stitches to 2 needles held to the outside—it may feel a bit awkward, but these 2 needles will be positioned parallel to each other with the 5 C stitches on a holder between them.

Round 3: With the live strand of B, kfb in each stitch—10 stitches.

Round 4: Join 2 new strands of C; hold the strands of C with the existing strand of B, and knit around—10 triple stitches.

Note: I found it easiest to work these stitches as C, C, B.

Transfer the 1st set of the C stitches to holders held to the center to work the medium petals. Slip the 2nd set of the C stitches onto a needle, and transfer the B stitches to holders held to the outside in groups of 2 to work the sepal leaves later. The needle should be held between the center C stitches and the outer B stitches.

Round 5: With one of the live strands of C, kfb in each stitch—20 stitches. Divide the stitches between 4 needles.

Round 6: Using both live strands of C held together, knit around—40 stitches (20 double stitches). Transfer every other C stitch to holders held to the outside of the center C stitches already on hold to make the large petals. Transfer the remaining C stitches to holders held just inside the B stitches to work the long outermost petals. Cut the strands of B and C and weave in the ends into the same color areas once the flower is complete.

✳

1ST SEPAL LEAF

Position the flower so that the peduncle is facing you and the flower center is facing away.

Transfer 2 B stitches from a holder to a needle.

Row 1: (RS): Join a new strand of B and kfb in each stitch—4 stitches.

Row 2: P4.

Row 3: K1, LI-R, k2, LI-L, k1—6 stitches.

Rows 4–6: Work in stockinette stitch.

Row 7: Ssk, k2, k2tog—4 stitches.

Row 8: P4.

Row 9: Ssk, k2tog—2 stitches.

Row 10: P2.

Row 11: Skp—1 stitch.

Cut the yarn and draw the tail through the last stitch to fasten off. Weave in the end on the wrong-side edge of the sepal leaf.

✳

2ND–5TH SEPAL LEAVES

Transfer the 2 B stitches to the left of the sepal just completed to a needle. Join a new strand of B and work as for the 1st sepal.

✳

PETALS

There are 4 rounds of C stitches now on holders. Begin with the stitches held outermost (the 1st round) and work in rounds toward the center.

Long Outermost Petals (make 5)

Of the 1st round's 20 C stitches on holders to the outside, transfer 4 stitches to a needle.

Row 1 (RS): With the flower center facing you and the peduncle facing away, join a new strand of C; k4.

Row 2: P4.

Row 3: K1, LI-R, k2, LI-L, k1—6 stitches.

Row 4: P6.

Row 5: K1, LI-R, knit to the last stitch, LI-L, k1—8 stitches.

Rows 6–14: Work in stockinette stitch.

Row 15: K3, ssk, k3—7 stitches.

Row 16: P7.

Row 17: Ssk, k3, k2tog—5 stitches.

Row 18: P5.

Row 19: Ssk, k1, k2tog—3 stitches.

Row 20: P3.

Row 21: Sk2p—1 stitch.

Cut the yarn and draw the tail through the remaining stitch to fasten off.

Weave in the ends at the base and apex of each petal along the wrong-side edges of the petal.

Work the remaining long outermost petals as for the 1st.

Large Petals (make 10)

As before, position the flower so that the center is facing you. Transfer 2 of the 2nd round's 20 C stitches on holders to a needle.

Row 1 (RS): Join a new strand of C; kfbf in each stitch— 6 stitches.

Row 2: P6.

Row 3: K1, LI-R, k4, LI-L, k1—8 stitches.

Rows 4–8: Work in stockinette stitch.

Row 9: Ssk, k4, k2tog—6 stitches.

Row 10: P6.

Row 11: Ssk, k2, k2tog—4 stitches.

Row 12: P2tog, ssp—2 stitches.

Row 13: Skp—1 stitch.

Cut the yarn and draw the tail through the remaining stitch to fasten off.

Weave in the ends at the base and apex of each petal along the wrong-side edges of the petal so that the petal tips are slightly rounded in appearance.

Work the remaining large petals as for the 1st.

Medium Petals (make 5)

With the flower center facing you, transfer 2 of the 3rd round's 10 C stitches on holders to a needle.

Row 1 (RS): Join a strand of C; kfb in each stitch—4 stitches.

Row 2: P4.

Row 3: K1, LI-R, k2, LI-L, k1—6 stitches.

Rows 4–9: Work in stockinette stitch.

Row 10: P2tog, p2, ssp—4 stitches.

Row 11: Ssk, k2tog—2 stitches.

Bind off purlwise.

Cut the yarn and weave in the ends on the underside of the petals so that the petal tips appear rounded.

Work the remaining medium petals as for the 1st.

Small Center Petals (make 3)

Set up for center petals: With the flower center facing you, transfer the 3 C stitches on holders at the center to a needle, join a new strand of C and k1, kfb, k1—4 stitches. Transfer these 4 stitches to a holder. Transfer the remaining 2 stitches to a needle, and use the live yarn to perform row 1. Once complete, the 3 center petals are arranged in a tiny circle—make sure that you orient the flower so that the knit side of each of these last 3 petals is facing inward toward the flower center.

Row 1 (RS): With the live yarn, kfb in each stitch—4 stitches.

Row 2: P4.

Row 3: K1, LI-R, k2, LI-L, k1—6 stitches.

Rows 4–8: Work in stockinette stitch.

Row 9: Ssk, k2, k2tog—4 stitches.

Row 10: P2tog, ssp—2 stitches.

Bind off knitwise.

Cut the yarn and weave in the ends along the underside edges of the petals so that the petal tips appear rounded.

Work the remaining small center petals as for the 1st.

✳

FINISHING

Before felting, tack sepal leaves to the underside of the outermost round of petals using a sharp needle, like-colored yarn, and invisible stitches.

If desired, wire petals after felting so that they curl inward toward the center. The pictured flower is not wired.

Giant White
Calla Lily

Zantedeschia aethiopica

DIFFICULTY LEVEL ✎ ✎ ✎ ✎

REQUIRED YARN COLORS

Green (A), white (B), and pale green
or yellow (C)

SAMPLE

Finished Measurements
Flower blossom height from stem to
petal tip: 6" (15cm)
Stem length: 11" (28cm)

Yarns Used
Universal Yarn *Deluxe Worsted*
Greenery #61633 (A), White #12257
(B), and Shadow Lime #71661 (C)

INSTRUCTIONS

PEDUNCLE (MAIN STEM)

With A, cast on 8 stitches.
I-Cord Round: Knit across; without
turning your work, slip the row to the
other end of the needle; pull the yarn
across the back to begin the next
round.
Repeat the I-cord round for 66 rounds
or desired length. Use a crochet
hook to latch up the loose loop on
the backside of the I-cord, creating
another stitch—9 stitches.

*

RECEPTACLE
(FLOWER FOUNDATION)

Round 1: With 2 strands of A, knit
around.
Transfer every other A stitch to holders held to the center for the pistil.
Transfer the remaining 9 A stitches to

2 needles held to the outside to work
the flower petal.

*

PETAL

Round 1: With the live (single) strand
of A, [k1, kfb] 4 times, k1—13
stitches.
Round 2: Knit around.
Turn to begin to work the petal in
rows to create the front opening in
the petal. Mark the beginning of the
row (the front opening) with a stitch
marker. Cut A and weave in the end
down the center of the peduncle.
Row 1 (WS): Change to B; p13, turn.
Row 2 (RS): Kfbf, kfb, knit to the last 2
stitches, kfb, kfbf—19 stitches.
Row 3: P19.
Row 4: Kfbf, kfb, k4, M1, k4, M1, k4,
M1, k4, kfb—26 stitches.
Row 5: P26.
Row 6: Kfb, knit to the last stitch,
kfb—28 stitches.
Row 7: [P7, place marker] 3 times,
p7.
Row 8: [Knit to the marker, M1, slip
marker] 3 times, knit to end—31
stitches.
Row 9: P31.
Rows 10 and 11: Work in stockinette
stitch.
Row 12: Kfb, [knit to the marker, M1,
slip marker] 3 times, knit to the last
stitch, kfb—36 stitches.
Row 13: P36.
Row 14: Kfb, knit to end—37 stitches.
Row 15: P37.
Row 16: Ssk, knit to the 1st marker,
M1, slip marker; knit to the next
marker, M1, slip marker, k1, M1; knit

to the last marker, M1, slip marker; knit
to the last stitch, k2tog—39 stitches.
Row 17: P39.
Row 18: Ssk, knit to the 2nd marker,
M1, slip marker, k1, M1, knit to the
last 2 stitches, k2tog—39 stitches.
Row 19: P2tog, purl to the last 2
stitches, ssp—37 stitches.
Row 20: Repeat row 16—39 stitches.
Row 21: Repeat row 19—37 stitches.
Row 22: Knit to the last 2 stitches,
k2tog—36 stitches.
Row 23: Repeat row 19—34 stitches.
Row 24: Ssk, [knit to the next marker,
M1, slip marker, k1, M1] twice, knit
to the last 2 stitches, remove marker,
k2tog—36 stitches.
Row 25: Repeat row 19—34 stitches.
Row 26: Knit to the 1st marker,
remove marker, knit to the 2nd
marker, M1, slip marker, k1, M1,
knit to the last 2 stitches, k2tog—35
stitches.
Row 27: Repeat row 19—33 stitches.
Row 28: Ssk, knit to the last 2 stitches,
k2tog—31 stitches.
Row 29: Repeat row 19—29 stitches.
Row 30: Ssk, knit to the marker, M1-r,
slip marker, k1, M1, knit to the last 2
stitches, k2tog—29 stitches.
Row 31: Purl to the last 2 stitches,
ssp—28 stitches.
Row 32: Sssk, knit to the marker, M1,
slip marker, k1, M1, knit to the last 3
stitches, k3tog—26 stitches.
Row 33: P3tog, purl to last 3 stitches,
sssp—22 stitches.
Row 34: Sssk, knit to the marker, M1,
remove marker, k1, M1, knit to the
end—22 stitches.
Row 35: Purl to the last 2 stitches,
ssp—21 stitches.

Row 36: Sssk, knit to the last 3 stitches, k3tog—17 stitches.

Row 37: Repeat row 33—13 stitches.

Row 38: Sssk, knit to the end—11 stitches.

Row 39: P2tog, purl to the last 3 stitches, sssp—8 stitches.

Row 40: K8.

Row 41: P2tog, purl to the end—7 stitches.

Row 42: Sssk, knit to the end—5 stitches.

Row 43: P3, ssp—4 stitches.

Row 44: Ssk, k2—3 stitches.

Row 45: P3.

Row 46: K1, k2tog—2 stitches.

Row 47: P2.

Row 48: Skp—1 stitch.

Row 49: P1.

Row 50: K1.

Cut the yarn and draw through the remaining stitch to fasten.

Weave in the end along the wrong-side edge of the petal.

*

PISTIL

Transfer the 9 A stitches to 2 needles.

Round 1: Join a strand of C; k1, [k2tog] 4 times—5 stitches. Consolidate the stitches on 1 needle.

Rounds 2–7: Knit as an I-cord.

Round 8: K2tog, k3—4 stitches.

Rounds 9–12: Knit as an I-cord.

Round 13: K2tog, k2—3 stitches.

Rounds 14–16: Knit as an I-cord.

Cut the yarn. Draw the tail through the remaining 3 stitches to fasten off. Weave the end down into pistil.

FINISHING

Use like-colored yarn or sewing thread and a sharp needle and use invisible stitches to tack the flower front closed: With the front of the flower facing you, cross the left front over the right (or the other way if you prefer—I've looked at a lot of calla lilies and they cross either way, though I have made the left front a little frillier). Angle the fronts so that the flute of the petal is narrow at the bottom and flares at the top. Tack the flower closed in a way that utilizes the natural curl of the knitting to mimic the curling front of the calla lily. I found that felting the calla lily smoothes out the uneven surface created by all the shaping in this flower.

Wire the petal and peduncle *after* felting.

Hollyhock

Alcea rosea

DIFFICULTY LEVEL 🌿 🌿 🌿 🌿

REQUIRED YARN COLORS

Green (A), pale yellow (B), medium or dark red (C), and Crystal Palace *Fizz* in yellow (D)

SAMPLES

Finished Measurements
Flower blossom diameter: 7" (18cm)
Stem length: 17" (43cm)

Yarns Used
Stonehedge Fiber Mill *Shepherd's Wool* (worsted weight) Lime (A), Spring Chick Yellow (B), and Garnet (C); and Lime (A), Spring Chick Yellow (B), and Berries (C)
Crystal Palace *Fizz* Sunshine (#7305) (D)

INSTRUCTIONS

PEDUNCLE (MAIN STEM) & PEDICELS (BRANCHING STEMS)

With A, cast on 3 stitches.

I-Cord Round: Knit across; without turning your work, slip the row to the other end of the needle; pull the yarn across the back to begin the next round.

Repeat the I-cord round for 36 rounds or desired length.

Setup round for the 1st pedicel: [kfb] 3 times—6 stitches.

Next round: K3; k3 and then put these 3 stitches on the needle for the peduncle and 3 stitches on a holder for the 1st pedicel.

Work the stitches as an I-cord for

another 30 rounds.

Work the setup round for the 2nd pedicel as for the first. Work the peduncle stitches as an I-cord for another 24 rounds.

✽

RECEPTACLE (FLOWER FOUNDATION)

Round 1: Kfb, k1, kfb—5 stitches. Some may want to divide the stitches between 2 needles here instead of after row 3 for greater ease of working.

Round 2: Knit around.

Round 3: Kfb in each stitch—10 stitches.

Divide the stitches between 2 needles.

Round 4: Knit around.

Round 5: Join 2 strands of B, hold together with A, and knit around.

Round 6: Transfer the 10 A stitches to holders held to the outside for sepal leaves; transfer every other B stitch to a needle held to the center for the pistil; transfer the remaining 10 B stitches to 5 holders held between the center B and the outside A stitches for the petals. Cut all strands of yarn. Tie like-colored yarns in square knots. Weave A strands down the peduncle, weave B strands into the pistil after it is formed.

✽

PISTIL

Transfer the 10 center B stitches to 2 needles, join a new strand of B and work the following rounds as for an I-cord.

Round 1: K2tog around—5 stitches.

Round 2: Join a strand of D and hold together with B to knit around.

Round 3: K2tog, k1, k2tog—3 stitches.

Rounds 4 and 5: Knit around.

Round 6: Kfb around—6 stitches. Divide between 2 needles for greater ease of working.

Round 7: Knit around. Cut the strand of D and weave in the end down the pistil center.

Round 8: K2tog around—3 stitches. Cut the yarn and draw the tail through the remaining 3 stitches to fasten off.

Weave in the end down the pistil center.

✽

SEPAL LEAVES

Transfer the 10 A sepal stitches to 2 needles.

Round 1: [K1, kfb] 5 times—15 stitches.

Round 2: Knit around. Cut the yarn, tie the A ends in a square knot and weave the ends into the foundation to secure. Leave 3 stitches on a needle and transfer the remaining 12 stitches to holders in groups of 3.

1st Sepal Leaf

Position the flower so that the pistil is facing you and the pedicel and peduncle are facing away from you. Join a new strand of A.

Row 1 (WS): Purl across the needle holding 3 stitches.

Row 2 (RS): K1, M1-R, k1, M1-L, k1—5 stitches.

Row 3: P5.

Row 4: Ssk, k1, k2tog—3 stitches.

Row 5: P3.

Row 6: Sk2p—1 stitch.

Row 7: P1.

Cut the yarn and pull the tail through the remaining stitch.

Weave in the ends at the base and the apex of the sepal leaf along the wrong side of the leaf edges.

2nd–5th Sepal Leaves

Transfer the 3 stitches to the left of the leaf just completed to their own needle. Join a new strand of A and work as for the 1st leaf.

*

PETALS

Position the flower so that the pistil is facing you.

Transfer the remaining 10 B stitches to 3 needles. Join a new strand of B and knit around.

Round 1: [K2, M1] 5 times—15 stitches.

Round 2: Knit around. Cut the yarn, tie the B ends in a square knot and weave into the receptacle to secure. Leave 3 stitches on a needle and transfer the remaining 12 stitches to holders in groups of 3.

*

1ST PETAL

Row 1 (RS): Change to C and kfb in each stitch—6 stitches.

Row 2: P6.

Row 3: [Kfb] twice, knit to the last 2 stitches, [kfb] twice—10 stitches.

Row 4: Purl across.

Rows 5–10: Repeat [rows 3 and 4] 3 times—22 stitches.

Rows 11–20: Work in stockinette stitch.

Row 21: Ssk, knit to the last 2 stitches, k2tog—20 stitches. Mark both ends of this row.

Row 22: Purl across.

Rows 23 and 24: Repeat rows 21 and 22—18 stitches. Do not bind off. Cut the strand of C and use it for the pickup row below.

Pickup Row (RS): With the right side facing you, beginning at the marker on the right edge of the petal, pick up and knit 5 stitches along the right edge, knit 18 stitches across the live stitches at the top, pick up and knit 5 stitches along the left edge to the marker, turn—28 stitches.

Picot Bind-off Row (WS): Using a cable cast-on method, *cast on 2 stitches, then bind off 3 stitches knitwise. Slip the remaining stitch from the right-hand needle onto the left-hand needle; repeat from * until all stitches are bound off.

*

2ND–5TH PETALS

Transfer the 3 stitches to the left of the petal just completed to a needle. Join a new strand of C and work as for the 1st petal.

*

PEDICELS (BRANCHING STEMS)

Transfer the 3 A Peduncle stitches on hold to a needle.

Round 1: Join a new strand of A and knit as an I-cord—3 stitches.

Work each flower as for the main flower, beginning with the receptacle.

*

FINISHING

Use like-colored yarn or sewing thread and a sharp needle to tack the petals together so that the flower forms a teacup shape. As is customary with hollyhocks, always position the right side edge of the petal (as you look down into the center of the flower) so that it overlaps the petal to its right.

The hollyhock flowers benefit greatly from wiring the peduncle, pedicels, and petals.

Japanese Anemone

Anemone hybrida

REQUIRED YARN COLORS

Green (A), yellow-green (B), white or pink (C), and lighter-gauge yarn in yellow (D)

SAMPLE

Finished Measurements
Flower head diameter: 3" (7.5cm)
Stem length: 12" (30.5cm)

Yarns Used
Stonehedge Fiber Mill *Shepherd's Wool* (worsted weight) Lime (A), Spring Green (B), Zinnia Pink (C), and (fingering weight) Spring Chick (D)

INSTRUCTIONS

PEDUNCLE (MAIN STEM)

With A, cast on 3 stitches.

I-Cord Round: Knit across; without turning your work, slip the row to the other end of the needle; pull the yarn across the back to begin the next round.

Repeat the I-cord round for 72 rounds or desired length.

*

FOUNDATION FOR FLOWER CENTER & PETALS

Round 1: Kfb in each stitch—6 stitches.

Divide the stitches between 2 needles.

Round 2: Join strands of B and C; with A, B, and C held together, knit around.

Round 3: Transfer the 6 A stitches to holders held to the outside for the sepal leaves; slip the 6 B stitches onto needles held to the center for the pistil; transfer the 6 C stitches to holders held between the A and B stitches for the petals. Do not cut the yarns.

*

PISTIL

Round 1: Using the 6 B stitches and the live strand of B, [k1, kfb, k1] twice—8 stitches.

Round 2: Knit around.

Round 3: [K2tog] 4 times—4 stitches. Cut the yarn, leaving an 8" (20.5cm) tail; draw the end through the 4 stitches to close.

Weave the end down the center and then around the 1st round of stitches, pulling the round tight as you do, so as to make the center into a tiny little round pillow in the flower center.

*

COROLLA (SETUP FOR PETALS)

Transfer the 6 C stitches to 2 parallel needles. Position the flower so that the peduncle is facing you and the pistil is facing away.

Round 1: Join another strand of C; with the 2 strands of C held together, purl around, W&T—6 double stitches, 12 loops.

Round 2: With a single strand of C and working in the opposite direction, knit into each loop of the double stitches individually—12 stitches. If desired, divide the stitches between 3

needles for greater ease of working.

Round 3: With a double strand of C, knit around—12 double stitches, 24 loops. Cut the 2nd strand of C and weave in the end.

Transfer every other loop to 6 holders (2 stitches on each) held to the outside for the 2nd layer of petals; slip the remaining 12 stitches onto 3 or more needles held to the center for the 1st layer of petals.

*

1ST LAYER OF PETALS
1st Petal

With the pistil facing you, work the first 2 stitches of the round with the live strand of C.

Row 1 (RS): With a single strand of C, kfb in each stitch—4 stitches.

Row 2: P4.

Row 3: K1, LI-R, k2, LI-L, k1—6 stitches.

Rows 4–11: Work in stockinette stitch.

Row 12: P2tog, p2, ssp—4 stitches.

Row 13: K1, skp, k1—3 stitches.

Row 14: Bind off the 3 remaining stitches purlwise on the wrong side. Cut the yarn; weave in the ends at the base and apex of the petal along the underside edge of the petal.

2nd–5th Petals

Transfer the 2 stitches to the left of the petal just completed to a needle.

Join a new strand of C and work as for the 1st petal.

2ND LAYER OF PETALS

Transfer 2 of the 12 C stitches held to the outside to 3 needles, with the petal stitches being offset by 1 stitch from the 1st layer of petals so that this layer is not directly underneath the 1st layer. Work as for the 1st layer of petals.

*

SEPAL LEAVES

Transfer the 6 A stitches to 2 needles. Position the flower so that the peduncle is facing you and the flower center facing away.

With the live strand of A and using the backwards-loop method, *cast on 3 stitches, then bind off 4; slip the remaining stitch from the right-hand needle onto the left-hand needle; repeat from * until all 6 stitches have been bound off.

Cut the yarn and weave in the end so that the first and last sepal leaf sit snugly next to each other.

*

STAMENS

Cut 10 strands of D 3" (7.5cm) long, adjusting strand length for smaller- or larger-gauge flowers. Refer to the instructions for making stamens (page 30). Trim the strands to approximately ¼"–⅜" (6–10mm) or an appropriately scaled length.

Jasmine

Jasminum officinale

DIFFICULTY LEVEL 🖊🖊🖊

REQUIRED YARN COLORS
Green (A) and white (B)

SAMPLE
Finished Measurements
Flower head diameter: 2" (5cm)
Stem length: 2" (5cm)

Yarns Used
Stonehedge Fiber Mill *Shepherd's Wool* (fingering weight) Spring Green or Lime Green (A) and White (B)

INSTRUCTIONS

PEDUNCLE (MAIN STEM)

With A, cast on 2 stitches.
I-Cord Round: Knit across; without turning your work, slip the row to the other end of the needle; pull the yarn across the back to begin the next round.
Repeat the I-cord round for 12 rounds or desired length.

✳

RECEPTACLE (FLOWER FOUNDATION) & COROLLA (SETUP FOR PETALS)

Round 1: Kfb in each stitch—4 stitches.
Round 2: Knit around.
Round 3: K2, M1, k2—5 stitches.
Round 4: With a strand of A and a strand of B held together, knit around. Transfer the 5 A stitches to 2 needles held to the outside. Transfer the 5 B

stitches to a holder held to the center.
Bind-off Round: Working in the round on the live A stitches and using the backwards-loop cast-on method (and still working in the round), *cast on 5 stitches; bind off 6 stitches; slip the remaining stitch from the right-hand needle onto the left-hand needle; repeat from * until all stitches are bound off.
Weave in the ends so that the first and last sepal leaf sit snugly next to each other.

Corolla

With the live strand of B, work as an I-cord for 5 rounds.
Round 6: K1, M1-R, k3, M1-L, k1—7 stitches. Divide stitches between 2 needles.
Round 7: Knit around.
Round 8: K2, M1-R, k1, kfb, k1, M1-L, k2—10 stitches. Divide stitches evenly between 2 needles.
Round 9: Purl around.
Transfer all but the last 2 stitches worked to holders in groups of 2.

✳

1ST PETAL

Row 1: Kfb in each stitch—4 stitches.
Row 2: P4.
Row 3: Kfb, k2, kfb—6 stitches.
Rows 4–10: Work in stockinette stitch.
Row 11: Ssk, k2, k2tog—4 stitches.
Row 12: P4.
Row 13: Ssk, k2tog—2 stitches. Cut the yarn and draw the end through the remaining 2 stitches to finish off. Weave in the ends on the petal underside edges.

2ND–5TH PETALS

Slip the 2 stitches to the left of the completed petal onto a needle. Join a new strand of B and work as for the 1st petal.

FINISHING

Stretch the little sepal leaves up around the corolla and tack using a sharp needle and lighter-gauge like-colored yarn or sewing thread.

Lesser Celandine

Ranunculus ficaria

DIFFICULTY LEVEL 🌱 🌱 🌱

REQUIRED YARN COLORS
Medium green (A), bright yellow (B),
and light green (C)

SAMPLE
Finished Measurements
Flower head diameter: 3½" (9cm)
Peduncle length: 4" (10cm)

Yarns Used
Stonehedge Fiber Mill *Shepherd's Wool*
(fingering weight) Lime Green (A),
Sun Yellow (B), and Spring Green (C)

PEDUNCLE
(MAIN STEM)

With A, cast on 3 stitches.

I-Cord Round: Knit across; without turning your work, slip the row to the other end of the needle; pull the yarn across the back to begin the next round.

Repeat the I-cord round for 18 rounds or desired length.

✳

RECEPTACLE
(FLOWER FOUNDATION)

Round 1: Join a new strand of A and a strand of B; with 2 strands of A and a single strand of B held together, knit around.

Transfer every other A stitch to a holder held to the outside for the sepal leaves. Transfer the remaining A stitches to a holder held to the center for the pistil; slip the 3 B stitches onto 2 double-pointed needles held to the outside of the center A stitches to continue the foundation. Cut the strands of A and weave in the ends down the center of the peduncle.

Round 2: With the live strand of B, kfb in each stitch around—6 stitches. Divide stitches evenly between the 2 needles.

Round 3: [K2, M1] 3 times; W&T— 9 stitches. Reposition the flower so the center is facing you and you are now working in the opposite direction.

Round 4 (RS): Kfb in each stitch— 18 stitches.

Round 5: Knit around.

1ST PETAL

Row 1 (RS): Continue as if in the round; k1, M1, k1—3 stitches. Transfer the remaining 16 stitches to 8 holders (2 stitches each) for the last 8 petals. Turn the work.

Row 2 (WS): P3.

Row 3: K1, LI-R, k1, LI-L, k1—5 stitches.

Rows 4–10: Work in stockinette stitch.

Row 11: Ssk, k1, k2tog—3 stitches.

Row 12: P3.

Row 13: Sk2p—1 stitch. Cut the yarn and draw the tail through the remaining stitch. Weave in the tail along the underside edge of the petal so that the petal tip appears rounded.

✳

2ND–9TH PETALS

Transfer the next 2 stitches to a needle. With the flower center facing you join a new strand of B and complete as for the 1st petal.

✳

PISTIL

Transfer the 3 center A stitches to a needle.

Join a strand of C and knit 2 rounds as for an I-cord.

Cut the yarn and draw the tail through the 3 stitches to fasten off. Weave the tail down into the center to secure.

✳

SEPAL LEAVES

Transfer the 3 A stitches held to the outside to 2 needles.

Round 1: Join a new strand of A and kfbf in each stitch—9 stitches.

Bind-off Round: Working in the round on the live A stitches and using the backwards-loop cast-on method (and still working in the round), *cast on 3 stitches; bind off 4 stitches; slip the remaining stitch from the right-hand needle onto the left-hand needle; repeat from * until all stitches are bound off.

Weave in the ends so that the first and last sepal leaf sit snugly next to each other.

✳

STAMENS

Cut 18 strands of B 3" (7.5cm) long, adjusting the strand length for smaller- or larger-gauge flowers. For instructions on making stamens refer to page 30. Trim the strands to approximately ½" (13mm) or appropriately scaled length.

Madagascar
Jasmine

Stephanotis floribunda

DIFFICULTY LEVEL ✐ ✐ ✐ ✐

REQUIRED YARN COLORS
Green (A) and white (B)

SAMPLES
Finished Measurements
Flower head diameter: 2½" (6.5cm)
Height from stem tip to flower: 4"
(10cm)

Yarns Used
Stonehedge Fiber Mill *Shepherd's Wool* (worsted weight) Lime (A)
and White (B)

<hr>

INSTRUCTIONS

PEDUNCLE (MAIN STEM)
With A, cast on 2 stitches.
I-Cord Round: Knit across; without turning your work, slip the row to the other end of the needle; pull the yarn across the back to begin the next round.
Repeat the I-cord round for 12 rounds or desired length.

*

RECEPTACLE (FLOWER FOUNDATION)
Round 1: Kfb, M1, kfb—5 stitches.
Round 2: Knit around.
Round 3: Kfb in each stitch—10 stitches.
Divide the stitches between 2 needles.
Round 4: Change to B. *K1, place the next stitch (unworked) on a holder held to the outside; repeat from * around—5 B stitches on 1 needle for

the receptacle, 5 unworked A stitches on 2–3 holders held to the outside for the sepals. Do not cut A.
Round 5: With live strand of B, k2, M1, k1, M1, k2—7 stitches.
Divide the stitches between 2 needles.
Round 6: K2, M1, k3, M1, k2—9 stitches.
Round 7: Knit around.
Round 8: Ssk, k2tog, k1, ssk, k2tog—5 stitches.
Put the stitches on 1 needle to work as for an I-cord.
Rounds 9–18: Knit.
Round 19: Kfb around—10 stitches.
Divide the stitches between 2 needles.
Round 20: Purl around.

*

1ST PETAL
Keep the last 2 stitches worked during round 20 on the needle to work the 1st petal; put the remaining 8 stitches on 4 holders (2 stitches each).
Position the flower so that the flower center is facing you and the peduncle is facing away from you.
Row 1 (RS): Using the live strand of B, k1, M1, k1—3 stitches.

Row 2: P3.
Row 3: K1, LI-R, k2—4 stitches.
Rows 4–6: Work in stockinette stitch.
Row 7: K1, skp, k1—3 stitches.
Cut the yarn and pull the tail through the remaining 3 stitches.
Weave in the ends at the base and apex of the petal.

*

2ND–5TH PETALS
Transfer the 2 stitches to the left of the petal just completed to a needle.
Join a new strand of B and work as for the 1st petal.

*

SEPALS
With the peduncle facing you, transfer the 5 sepal (A) stitches to 3 needles (arranged 1-2-2), putting the stitch to the left of the live yarn on its own needle.
Bind-off Round: Beginning with the single stitch, use the backwards-loop cast-on method to *cast 2 stitches onto the needle. Bind off the 2 cast-on stitches—1 stitch remains on the right-hand needle. Slip the next stitch from the left-hand needle (holding 2 stitches) onto the right-hand needle and bind off the 1st stitch by passing it over the slipped stitch. Slip the remaining stitch back onto the left-hand needle. Repeat from * until all 5 sepal stitches are bound off, then cut the yarn and fasten off the last stitch. Weave in the end so that the sepal leaves are placed evenly around the receptacle.

Meadowfoam

Limnanthes douglasii

DIFFICULTY LEVEL ◊ ◊ ◊ ◊

REQUIRED YARN COLORS

Green (A), yellow (B), white (C), and lighter-gauge golden yellow (D)

SAMPLE

Finished Measurements
Flower head diameter: 3½" (9cm)
Stem length: 2" (5cm)

Yarns Used
Plymouth *Galway Worsted* Happy Green #145 (A), Hot Neon Yellow #147 (B), and Natural #001 (C) Alpaca with a Twist *Fino* Yellow Ribbon #5010 (D)

PATTERN NOTE

When working across short rows, there's no need to hide the wraps.

INSTRUCTIONS

PEDUNCLE
(MAIN STEM)

With A, cast on 2 stitches.

I-Cord Round: Knit across; without turning your work, slip the row to the other end of the needle; pull the yarn across the back to begin the next round.

Repeat the I-cord round for 12 rounds or desired length.

RECEPTACLE
(FLOWER FOUNDATION)

Round 1: [Kfb] twice—4 stitches.
Round 2: Knit around.
Round 3: K2, M1, k2—5 stitches.
Divide the stitches between 2 needles.
Round 4: Join a strand of B; with A and B held together, knit around. Transfer the 5 A stitches to holders to the outside for the sepal leaves, keeping the 5 B stitches on the needles to continue working. Cut A and weave in the end down the peduncle center.
Round 5: With B, knit around.
Round 6: Purl around; W&T, reorienting the flower so that for the next 2 rounds, you will not only be working in the opposite direction, but the flower center will be facing you and the peduncle will be facing down.
Round 7: Going in the opposite direction, kfb in each stitch—10 stitches.
Round 8: Knit around. Cut the yarn and weave in the ends.
Transfer 8 stitches to 4 holders (2 stitches on each); keep 2 stitches on a needle to work the 1st petal.

✳

1ST PETAL

Position the flower so that the peduncle and petal underside are facing away and the flower center is facing you.

Row 1 (RS): Kfb, M1, kfb—5 sts.
Row 2: P5.
Row 3: K1, M1-R, k3, M1-L, k1—7 stitches.
Row 4: P7.
Row 5 (short row): K5, W&T.
Row 6 (short row): P3, W&T.

Row 7: K5.
Row 8: Change to C and purl across.
Rows 9 and 10: Work in stockinette stitch.
Row 11: K3, bind off 1, k3.
Row 12: *P3, turn, bind off. Cut the yarn and weave in the end so that the flower tip appears blunt and rounded; join a new strand and repeat from * for the other flower tip.

✳

2ND–5TH PETALS

Transfer the 2 stitches to the left of the petal just completed to a needle. Join a new strand of B and work as for the 1st petal.

✳

SEPAL LEAVES

Transfer the 5 A stitches to 2 needles. Join a new strand of A.

Bind-off Row: Using the backwards-loop cast-on method, *cast on 5 stitches and bind off 6; slip the remaining stitch from the right-hand onto the left-hand needle and repeat from * until all 5 stitches have been bound off. Cut the yarn and weave in the end so that the first and last sepal leaves sit snugly next to each other.

✳

STAMENS

Cut 5 strands of D 3" (7.5cm) long, adjusting the strand length for smaller- or larger-gauge flowers. Refer to page 30 for instructions on making stamens.

Orange
Blossom
Citrus sinensis

DIFFICULTY LEVEL 𝒮 𝒮 𝒮 𝒮

REQUIRED YARN COLORS

Light green (A), natural white (B), and lighter-gauge yarn in pale yellow or white (C)

SAMPLES

Finished Measurements

Flower head diameter: 2½" (6.5cm)

Stem length: 2½–5" (6.5–12.5cm)

Yarns Used

Stonehedge Fiber Mill *Shepherd's Wool* (worsted weight) Spring Green (A), White (B), and (fingering weight) White (C)

INSTRUCTIONS

PEDUNCLE (MAIN STEM)

With A, cast on 3 stitches.

I-Cord Round: Knit across; without turning your work, slip the row to the other end of the needle; pull the yarn across the back to begin the next round.

Repeat the I-cord round 16 rounds or desired length.

❋

ESTABLISH A 1ST PEDICEL (BRANCHING STEM)

Setup round: [Kfb] twice, k1—5 stitches.

Next round: K1, put the next stitch on a holder unworked, k1, put the next stitch on the same holder unworked, k1—3 stitches on needle, 2 stitches on a holder for the 1st branching stalk and flower (to be worked later). Work 10 rounds as a 3-stitch I-cord.

❋

ESTABLISH A 2ND PEDICEL

Setup round: K1, [kfb] twice—5 stitches.

Next round: K2, put the next stitch on a holder unworked, k1, put the next stitch on the same holder unworked—3 stitches on needle, 2 stitches on holder for 2nd branching stalk and flower (to be worked later). Continue working a 3-stitch I-cord for another 6 rounds.

❋

MAIN FLOWER

Receptacle (flower foundation)

Round 1: K1, M1, k1, M1, k1—5 stitches.

Round 2: Join a strand of B; with A and B held together, knit around. Transfer the 5 A stitches to a needle and hold in the center for the flower pistil; put the B stitches on 2 holders (2 stitches on one, 3 on another) held to the outside. Do not cut A, as you'll work the pistil next. Cut B and weave in the ends.

Pistil

Round 1: Use the live strand of A to work in the round as for an I-cord: Ssk, k1, k2tog—3 stitches.

Rounds 2 and 3: Knit around.

Round 4: K1, kfb, k1—4 stitches. Cut the yarn and pull the tail through the remaining 4 stitches—as though

still working in the round—to join the 1st stitch to the 4th. Weave the end down into the center to secure.

Receptacle (continued)

Transfer the 5 B stitches to 2 needles. Position the flower so that the pistil is facing you and the peduncle is facing down and away—the pistil will be between the 2 needles; the next few rounds may seem a bit awkward but not difficult.

Round 3: With a new strand of B, kfb in each stitch—10 stitches.

Round 4: Knit around.

Transfer the last 8 stitches worked in round 4 to 4 holders (2 stitches on each holder)—the first 2 stitches worked in round 2 remain on the needle.

1st Petal

Position the flower so that the pistil is facing you and the peduncle is facing down and away.

Row 1 (RS): K1, M1, k1—3 stitches.
Rows 2–6: Work in stockinette stitch.
Row 7: Sk2p—1 stitch.

Cut the yarn and pull the tail through the remaining stitch to fasten off. Weave in the end along the underside edge of the petal.

2nd–4th Petals

Transfer the next 2 stitches to a needle, join a new strand of B and work as for the 1st petal.

2ND FLOWER

Transfer the 2 stitches on the 1st holder on the peduncle to a needle.
Round 1: Join a strand of A; k1, M1, k1.

Continue working as a 3-stitch I-cord for 3 rounds.

Work as for the main flower.

*

3RD FLOWER

Transfer the 2 stitches on the remaining holder on the peduncle to a needle.
Round 1: Join a strand of A; k1, M1, k1.

Continue working as a 3-stitch I-cord for 6 rounds.

Work as for the main flower.

STAMENS

Cut eight 4" (10cm) strands of C, adjusting the strand length for smaller- or larger-gauge flowers. Refer to page 30 for instructions on making stamens. Trim stamens to ¼" (6.5cm) or an appropriately scaled length once complete.

——————— N O T E ———————

If worked in worsted-weight or lighter-gauge yarn, these flowers are small enough not to require wiring.

Oriental Lily

Lilium oriental 'Casablanca'

REQUIRED YARN COLORS

Medium green (A), spring green, (B), white (C), and lighter-gauge yarn in light green or white (D) and orangey-red (E)

SAMPLE

Finished Measurements
Flower blossom diameter: 8" (20.5cm)
Stem: 14" (35.5cm)

Yarns Used
Stonehedge Fiber Mill *Shepherd's Wool* (worsted weight) Lime Green (A), Spring Green (B), and White (C), and (fingering weight) Spring Green (D) and Red (E)

PATTERN NOTES

- The color changes in the petals should be worked as intarsia; use separate strands of yarn for the different colors. Interlock the yarns at the color changes to prevent holes.
- Requires needles approximately 5 sizes smaller for the pistil and stamen.

INSTRUCTIONS

PEDUNCLE
(MAIN STEM)

With A and the larger needles, cast on 4 stitches.
I-Cord Round: Knit across; without turning your work, slip the row to the other end of the needle; pull the yarn across the back to begin the next round.
Repeat the I-cord round for 109 rounds or desired length.

✻

RECEPTACLE
(FLOWER FOUNDATION)

Round 1: Change to B and knit around. Cut A and weave in the end.
Round 2: [K1, M1] 3 times, kfbf—9 stitches. Divide the stitches between 2 needles.
Round 3: With a strand of B and a strand of C held together, knit around. Slip all 9 C stitches onto holders held to the outside for the petals. Slip the B stitches onto holders as follows: Slip the 1st, 4th, and 7th B stitches onto a holder at the center for the pistil. Slip the remaining 6 stitches onto holders held between the C stitches and the center B stitches for the stamens. Cut C and tie the 2 ends together in a square knot to secure. Weave the ends into the petal underside edges after the petals have been created.

✻

PISTIL
Style

With D and the smaller needles, work the 3 center B stitches as an I-cord for 36 rounds.

Stigma
*Using the backwards-loop cast-on method, cast on 3 stitches, then bind off 4 stitches; slip the remaining stitch onto the left-hand needle and repeat from * twice, binding off the 3 center stitches. Cut A; then weave the end into the center of the pistil so that the 1st and 3rd nodes of the stigma sit snugly next to each other.

✻

STAMENS

Transfer the 6 B stitches from holders to 2 smaller needles. Join a new strand of D and, working in the round, kfb in each stitch—12 stitches. Transfer all but the last 2 stitches to holders in groups of 2 for the filaments.

1st Filament

Knit the 2 stitches as an I-cord for 24 rounds.

Next round: K2tog—1 stitch.

Anther

Change to E; slip the stitch onto the other end of the needle and k1. Tie the ends of D and E in a square knot. Weave the ends into like-colored fields after the anther has been finished.

With E and using the backwards-loop cast-on method, cast on 8 stitches. Bind off all but 1 stitch. Using the backwards-loop cast-on method, cast on 8 stitches in the opposite direction. Bind off the remaining stitches. Cut the yarn. Weave in the end so that you minimize the slight jog between the 2 halves of the anther.

2nd–6th Filaments

Transfer the 2 stitches to the left of the filament just completed to a smaller needle. Join a new strand of D and work as for the 1st filament and anther.

*

PETALS

Orient the flower so that the pistil is facing up toward you and the peduncle is facing down.

Transfer the 9 C stitches to 3 larger needles and kfb in each stitch around—18 stitches.

Cut C. Tie the 2 C ends in a square knot. Weave in the ends on the underside edges of the petal after the petals have been created.

Transfer all but the first 3 stitches to holders in groups of 3.

1st Large Front Petal

Row 1 (RS): Join a strand of C and kfb; join a strand of B and kfbf; join a new strand of C and kfb—7 stitches.
Row 2: C: P2; B: k3; C: p2.
Row 3: C: [Kfb] twice; B: p3; C: [kfb] twice—11 stitches.
Row 4: C: P4; B: k3; C: p4.
Row 5: C: [Kfb] twice, k2; B: p3; C: k2, [kfb] twice—15 stitches.
Row 6: C: P6; B: k3; C: p6.
Row 7: C: Kfb, k5; B: p3; C: k5, kfb—17 stitches.
Row 8: C: P7; B: k3; C: p7.
Row 9: C: Kfb, k6; B: p3; C: k6, kfb—19 stitches.
Rows 10–12: Work even.
Row 13: C: Kfb, k6, ssk; B: p1; C: k2tog, k6, kfb.
Row 14: C: P9; B: k1; C: p9.
Row 15: C: K1, ssk, k6; B: p1; k6, k2tog, k1—17 stitches.
Row 16: C: P8; B: k1; C: p8.
Row 17 (decrease row): C: K1, ssk, knit to the last 3 stitches, k2tog, k1—15 stitches. (Make sure you also knit the center stitch for row 17 only.) Cut B and the 2nd strand of C. Weave in the ends on the petal underside or same-color-field edges.
Row 18: P7, k1, p7.
Rows 19–42: Maintaining the established pattern, repeat the decrease row on rows 27, 35, 37, 39, and 41—5 stitches.
Row 43: Ssk, k1, k2tog—3 stitches.
Row 44: P3.
Row 45: Sk2p—1 stitch.
Cut the yarn and pull the end through the remaining stitch to fasten off. Weave the end in on the petal underside edge.

1st Narrow Back Petal

Transfer the 3 stitches to the left of the petal just worked to a larger needle.

Row 1 (RS): Join a strand of C and kfb; join a strand of B and kfbf; join a new strand of C and kfb—7 stitches.
Row 2: C: P2; B: k3; C: p2.
Row 3: C: Kfb, k1; B: p3; C: k1, kfb—9 stitches.
Row 4: C: P3; B: k3; C: p3.
Row 5: C: Kfb, k2; B: p3; C: k2, kfb—11 stitches.
Rows 6–12: Work even.
Row 13: C: Kfb, k2, ssk; B: p1; C: k2tog, k2, kfb.
Row 14: C: P5; B: k1; C: p5.
Rows 15 and 16: Work even.
Row 17: C: K11. Cut B and the 2nd strand of C and weave in the ends.
Row 18: P5, k1, p5.
Rows 19–30: Work even.
Row 31: K1, ssk, k2, p1, k2, k2tog, k1—9 stitches.
Row 32: P4, k1, p4.
Row 33: K1, ssk, k1, p1, k1, k2tog, k1—7 stitches.
Rows 34–36: Work even.
Row 37: K1, ssk, p1, k2tog, k1—5 stitches.
Row 38: P2, k1, p2.
Row 39: Ssk, k1, k2tog—3 stitches.
Row 40: P3.
Row 41: Sk2p—1 stitch.
Cut the yarn and pull the end through the remaining stitch to fasten off. Weave the end in on the petal underside edge.

3rd–6th Petals

Continue to alternate working a large front petal and a narrow back petal using the remaining 12 C stitches.

FINISHING

The finished flower should be tacked so that the large petals sit in front of the smaller petals. Use like-colored yarn or sewing thread and a needle to tack the large petals together at their widest points. This will cause the flower to cup somewhat. Tack the smaller petals to the larger petals. For best results, wire the petals, stamens, and pistil using 28-gauge brass or beading wire.

Refer to the instructions on page 32 for wiring the petals, pistil, and stamens. In this particular case, the pistil should have a slight curve to it. The stamens should curve slightly away from the pistil. The petals themselves should curve up and then slightly down and away from the center. Use images of actual lilies or the picture to guide your efforts.

Pansy

Viola tricolor

REQUIRED YARN COLORS
Green (A), yellow (B), and purple (C)

SAMPLE
Finished Measurements
Flower blossom width at widest point:
2¾" (7cm); blossom height: 3¾"
(9.5cm)
Stem length: 4" (10cm)

Yarns Used
Flower 1: Stonehedge Fiber Mill
Shepherd's Wool (worsted weight)
Lime (A), Sun Yellow (B), and Lilac (C)
Flower 2: Stonehedge Fiber Mill
Shepherd's Wool (worsted weight)
Spring Green (A), Sun Yellow (B),
and Purple (C)

INSTRUCTIONS

PEDUNCLE (MAIN STEM)
With A, cast on 2 stitches.
I-Cord Round: Knit across; without
turning your work, slip the row to the
other end of the needle; pull the yarn
across the back to begin the next
round. Repeat the I-cord round for 30
rounds or desired length.

✳

RECEPTACLE
(FOUNDATION FOR PETALS)
Round 1: Kfb in each stitch—4 stitches.
Round 2: Change to B; knit around.
Cut A and weave in the end down the
peduncle center.
Round 3: Kfb in each stitch—8 stitches.

Divide the stitches between 2 needles.
Round 4: Kfb in each stitch—16
stitches.

✳

PETALS
Keep the stitches on double-pointed
needles, or (for greater ease of working) with the right side facing up and
the peduncle of the flower pointing
down, transfer all but the 6 stitches
to the left of the live yarn to holders.
Do not cut B.

1st Large Upper Petal
Row 1 (RS): With the flower center
facing you—that is, the 6 stitches
are on a needle held in your left
hand with the flower's actual center
between you and the 6 live stitches—
change to C; [k1, transfer 1 stitch
unworked to a holder held to the
back] 3 times—3 stitches on a needle
in front and 3 stitches unworked on
a holder at back for the 2nd large
upper petal.
Row 2: P3.
Row 3: Kfb in each stitch—6 stitches.
Row 4: P6.
Row 5: K1, M1-R, k1, M1-R, k2,
M1-L, k1, M1-L, k1—10 stitches.
Row 6: P10.
Row 7: K1, M1-R, k8, M1-L, k1—12
stitches.
Rows 8–16: Work in stockinette stitch.
Row 17: Ssk, k8, k2tog—10 stitches.
Row 18: P10.
Row 19: [Ssk] twice, k2, [k2tog]
twice—6 stitches.
Bind off all stitches and weave in the
ends along the petal underside edges.

2nd Large Upper Petal
Transfer the 3 stitches on the holder
behind the 1st large petal to a needle
with the one completed petal on top
and held forward and the flower center facing you. The stitches on hold are
between you and the flower center.
Row 1 (RS): Join a new strand of C
and k3.
Complete as for the 1st large upper
petal.

Two Small Upper Petals
Transfer the 2 stitches on either side
of the large petals to 1 needle—4
stitches. The 2 large petals are farthest away from you with the flower
center between you and the 4 live
stitches on the needle.
Row 1 (RS): With B (still attached and
coming from slightly behind and to
the right), k4.
Row 2: P4.
Split the stitches: [Slip 1, transfer 1
stitch unworked to a holder held to
the back] twice—2 stitches on a needle in front to continue the 1st small
upper petal and 2 stitches unworked
on a holder at back for the 2nd small
upper petal.
Row 3: With B, kfbf in each stitch—6
stitches.
Row 4: P6.
Row 5: K1, M1-R, k4, M1-L, k1—8
stitches.
Row 6: P8.
Rows 7–10: Work in stockinette stitch.
Row 11: Ssk, k4, k2tog—6 stitches.
Row 12: P6.
Row 13: Ssk, k2, k2tog—4 stitches.
Bind off, cut the yarn and weave in
the ends.

2nd Small Upper Petal

Transfer the 2 stitches held in back to a needle. Join a new strand of B and work rows 3–13.

Single Lower Petal

Transfer the 6 remaining B stitches to a needle. Position the flower so that the worked petals are closest to you with the flower center between you and the live stitches on the needle.

Row 1 (RS): Join a strand of B; k1, [kfb] 4 times, k1—10 stitches.

Row 2: P10.

Row 3: K1, M1-R, k8, M1-L, k1—12 stitches.

Rows 4–8: Work in stockinette stitch.

Row 9: K1, ssk, k6, k2tog, k1—10 stitches.

Row 10: P1, p2tog, p4, ssp, p1—8 stitches.

Row 11: K1, ssk, k2, k2tog, k1 and *at the same time* bind off.

Cut the yarn and weave in the ends.

FINISHING

Using a tapestry needle and like-colored yarn, tack the 2 upper petals together so that they overlap in the center. Tack the 2 smaller upper petals to the large upper petals. You may also want to tack the lower petal to the upper petals in such a way that the flower petal forms a cup shape and stands out somewhat from the plane of the upper petals. Use photographs of actual pansies to inspire your shaping efforts.

EMBROIDERY

Use a lighter-gauge yarn to embroider detail on the pansy face.

Look at images of actual pansies to get inspired to come up with beautiful color combinations. For intarsia enthusiasts or those wishing to learn on a small scale, pansies are a veritable playground for different colorways.

Pawpaw
Blossom
Asimina triloba

DIFFICULTY LEVEL 𝟀 𝟀 𝟀 𝟀

REQUIRED YARN COLORS
Moss green (A) and wine red (B)

SAMPLE
Finished Measurements
Flower head diameter: 3½" (9cm)
Stem length: 1" (2.5cm)

Yarns Used
Stonehedge Fiber Mill *Shepherd's Wool*
(worsted weight) Spring Green (A)
and Berries (B)

INSTRUCTIONS

PEDUNCLE (MAIN STEM)

With A, cast on 3 stitches.

I-Cord Round: Knit across; without turning your work, slip the row to the other end of the needle; pull the yarn across the back to begin the next round.

Repeat the I-cord round for 6 rounds or desired length.

❋

RECEPTACLE (FLOWER FOUNDATION)

Round 1: Kfb around as for an I-cord—6 stitches.

Divide the stitches between 2 needles.

Round 2: Join another strand of A and a strand of B; holding the 2 strands of A and 1 strand of B together, knit around.

Transfer 6 A stitches to 2 needles held to the center for the pistil and the remaining 6 A stitches to 3

separate holders held to the outside (2 stitches on each) for the sepal leaves. Slip the 6 B stitches onto 3 holders (2 stitches on each) held between the outside A stitches and the center A stitches for the continuation of the receptacle below. Do not cut the yarns.

❋

PISTIL

Round 1: Using the live strand of A, [k1, k2tog] twice—4 stitches. Consolidate the stitches on 1 needle.

Rounds 2 and 3: Knit around as for an I-cord.

Cut the yarn and pull the tail through the remaining 4 stitches to fasten off. Weave the end down into the pistil to secure.

❋

1ST SEPAL LEAF

With the cast-on end of the peduncle facing you, transfer the first 2 A sepal stitches to the left of the live yarn to a needle.

Row 1 (RS—stem facing you): With the live strand of A, [kfb] twice—4 stitches.

Row 2: P4.

Row 3: K2, M1, k2—5 stitches.

Row 4: P5.

Row 5: Ssk, k1, k2tog—3 stitches.

Row 6: P3tog—1 stitch.

Cut the yarn, leaving a long tail, and pull the tail through the remaining stitch. After petals are created, use the tail to tack the sepal leaf to the intersection between the 2 large petals.

2ND & 3RD SEPAL LEAVES

Join a new strand of A and complete as for 1st sepal leaf.

❋

RECEPTACLE (CONTINUED)

Transfer the 6 B stitches to 2 double-pointed needles. Position the flower so that the stem is facing you.

Round 3: With the live strand of B, [kfbf, kfb] 3 times—15 stitches.

Transfer the stitches to 6 holders in 2 different colors so that there are 3 groups of 2 stitches that line up with the sepal leaves (these will become the small petals) and 3 groups of 3 stitches that fall between the sepal leaves (these will become the large petals).

Cut the yarn and weave in the ends. Doing this will add structure to the flower foundation.

❋

1ST LARGE PETAL

Transfer 1 set of 3 stitches to a needle.

Row 1 (RS—center facing you): Join a new strand of B; kfb, M1-R, k1, M1-L, kfb—7 stitches.

Row 2: P3, k1, p3.

Row 3: Kfb, k2, p1, k2, kfb—9 stitches.

Row 4: P4, k1, p4.

Row 5: Kfb, k3, p1, k3, kfb—11 stitches.

Rows 6–8: Work in the established stitch pattern.

Row 9: Ssk, k3, p1, k3, k2tog—9

stitches.

Row 10: P4, k1, p4.

Row 11: Ssk, k2, p1, k2, K2tog—7 stitches.

Row 12: P2tog, p1, k1, p1, ssp—5 stitches.

Row 13: Ssk, k1, k2tog—3 stitches.

Row 14: P3.

Row 15: Sk2p—1 stitch.

Cut the yarn and pull the tail through the remaining stitch to fasten off.

Weave in the ends at the apex and base of the petal along the underside edge of the petal.

*

2ND & 3RD LARGE PETALS

Work as for 1st large petal.

SMALL PETALS

Transfer 1 set of 2 stitches to a needle.

Row 1 (RS—center facing you): Join a new strand of B; kfb, M1, kfb—5 stitches.

Row 2: P2, k1, p2.

Row 3: Kfb, k1, p1, k1, kfb—7 stitches.

Rows 4–6: Work in the established stitch pattern.

Row 7: Ssk, k1, p1, k1, k2tog—5 stitches.

Row 8: P2, k1, p2.

Row 9: Ssk, p1, k2tog—3 stitches.

Row 10: P3.

Row 11: Sk2p—1 stitch.

Cut the yarn and pull the tail through the remaining stitch to fasten off.

Weave in the ends at the apex and base of the petal along the underside edge of the petal.

*

FINISHING

Using like-colored yarn or sewing thread and a sharp needle, tack the petals so that the widest parts of the large petals are connected. Doing this will make the petals "cup."

Tack the sepal leaves so that they curl upward around the outside of the flower, with the sepal leaf apex lining up with the tip of the small petals.

Periwinkle
Vinca major

DIFFICULTY LEVEL 🖊🖊🖊🖊

REQUIRED YARN COLORS
Medium green (A) and light lavender (B)

SAMPLE
Finished Measurements
Flower head diameter: 1½" (3.8cm)
Stem length: 2" (5cm)

Yarns Used
Stonehedge Fiber Mill *Shepherd's Wool* (worsted weight) Lime Green (A) and Lilac (B)

PATTERN NOTE
When working across short rows, there is no need to hide the wraps.

PEDUNCLE
(MAIN STEM)

With A, cast on 3 stitches.

I-Cord Round: Knit across; without turning your work, slip the row to the other end of the needle; pull the yarn across the back to begin the next round.

Repeat the I-cord round for 12 rounds or desired length.

*

RECEPTACLE
(FLOWER FOUNDATION) & SETUP FOR SEPAL LEAVES & COROLLA

Round 1: Kfb, k1, kfb—5 stitches.

Round 2: Join a new strand of A. With 2 strands of A held together, knit around.

Transfer every other A stitch to 2 needles held to the outside to work the sepal leaves. Transfer the remaining stitches to a holder held to the center to work the corolla.

*

SEPAL LEAVES

Round 1: With the live strand of A, knit around. You will be working *around* the stitches for the corolla. This is a little awkward, but not difficult.

Bind-off Round: Using the backwards-loop cast-on method (and still working in the round), *cast on 5 stitches; bind off 6 stitches; slip the remaining stitch from the right-hand needle onto the left-hand needle; repeat from * until all stitches are bound off.

Cut A, leaving a tail that is long enough to attach the first sepal leaf to the last as you weave in the ends.

*

COROLLA

Transfer the 5 center A stitches to 2 needles.

Join a strand of B and work 2 rounds in the same manner as the stem; that is, in the round as an I-cord.

Round 3: K2, kfb, k1, kfb—7 stitches.

Rounds 4–6: Knit around.

Round 7: K3, kfb, k3—8 stitches.

Round 8: [K2, M1, k2] twice—10 stitches.

Round 9: Purl around.

Keep the 2 stitches worked last during round 9 on the needle for the 1st petal; transfer the remaining 8 stitches to holders in groups of 2.

*

1ST PETAL

Position the flower so that the center is facing you.

Row 1 (RS): K1, M1, k1—3 stitches.

Row 2: P3.

Row 3: Kfb, k1, kfb—5 stitches.

Row 4: P5.

Row 5 (short row): K3, W&T.

Row 6: P3.

Row 7: K5.

Row 8: P5.

Row 9: Ssk, k3—4 stitches.

Row 10: Bind off purlwise on the wrong side. Cut the yarn and fasten off. Weave in the end along the underside edge of the petal so that the petal tips appear slightly rounded at the edges.

*

2ND–5TH PETALS

Transfer the 2 stitches to the left of the petal just completed to a needle. Join a new strand of B and work as for the 1st petal.

——————— NOTE ———————

It may be necessary to wire the petals if the flower is worked at a gauge larger than worsted weight.

————————————————————

Pheasant's Eye Daffodil

Narcissus poeticus

REQUIRED YARN COLORS

Medium green (A), apricot (B), white (C), lighter-gauge yarn in light yellow (D), and red (E)

SAMPLE

Finished Measurements
Flower head diameter: 6" (15cm)
Stem length: 10" (25.5cm)

Yarns Used
Stonehedge Fiber Mill *Shepherd's Wool* (worsted weight) Lime (A), Creamsicle (B), White (C), and (fingering weight) Spring Chick (D) and Red (E)
Smaller double-pointed needles for the ruffly edges of the flute

PATTERN NOTE

Requires needles approximately 5 sizes smaller for the pistil, stamen, and ruffly edges of the flute.

INSTRUCTIONS

PEDUNCLE
(MAIN STEM)

With A, cast on 5 stitches.

I-Cord Round: Knit across; without turning your work, slip the row to the other end of the needle; pull the yarn across the back to begin the next round.

Repeat the I-cord round for 36 rounds or desired length.

Next round: K2, ssk, k1—4 stitches. Continue to work as an I-cord for 12 more rounds.

Next round: Ssk, k2—3 stitches. Continue to work as an I-cord for 12 more rounds.

*

RECEPTACLE
(FLOWER FOUNDATION)

Round 1: Kfb in each stitch—6 stitches.
Divide the stitches between 2 needles.
Rounds 2–5: Knit around.
Round 6: [K1, k2tog] twice—4 stitches.
Rounds 7–10: Knit around.
Round 11: K2, M1, k2—5 stitches.
Rounds 12–14: Knit around.
Round 15: K1, M1, k4—6 stitches.
Rounds 16–18: Knit around. Cut A and weave in the ends down the peduncle.
Round 19: Join strands of B, C, and D. With these 3 strands held together, knit around. Transfer 6 C stitches to 3 holders held to the outside to work the petals; slip the 6 D stitches onto 1 smaller-gauge needle held to the center to work the stamens; transfer the 6 B stitches to 3 holders between the outer C stitches and the center D stitches to work the corolla. Do not cut yarns.

*

STAMEN ANTHERS

The *Narcissus poeticus* pistil is almost too tiny to be seen, but the anthers at the end of the stamen filament are quite noticeable: 3 filaments are long and 3 are short, giving the impression

that 3 anthers float above their counterparts.

Bind-off Round: With the live strand of B and the backwards-loop cast-on method, *cast 5 stitches onto the needle, bind off 6; slip the remaining stitch from the right-hand needle onto the left-hand needle; cast on 2 stitches, bind off 3; repeat from * twice more.

Cut the yarn; weave in the end by sewing it through the base of each anther in order to pull them together into the center. Make sure the first and last anther sit snugly next to each other.

*

TRUMPET

Transfer the 6 B stitches to 3 larger-gauge needles. With the live yarn, wrap the 1st stitch of the round and turn. Position the flower so that the flower center is facing you.

Round 1 (RS): Knit around in the opposite direction.
Round 2: *K1, M1, k1; repeat from * twice more—9 stitches.
Round 3: *K3, M1; repeat from * twice more—12 stitches.
Rounds 4–6: Knit around.
Round 7: Change to E and, using a smaller-gauge needle to work the stitches, kfbf in each stitch—36 stitches.
Round 8: Kfb in each stitch—72 stitches.
Bind-off Round: Using a cable cast-on method, *cast on 2 stitches, then bind off 3 stitches; slip the remaining stitch from the right-hand needle onto

the left-hand needle; repeat from * until all stitches are bound off. Cut the yarn and weave in the ends so that the first and last stitch of the round sit snugly next to each other.

*

COROLLA
(BASE FOR ALL PETALS)

Transfer the 6 C stitches to 2 or 3 needles. With the live yarn, wrap the 1st stitch of the round and turn. Position the flower so that the flower center is facing you.

Round 1: Kfbf in each stitch—18 stitches.

Round 2: Knit around.

Keep the last 3 stitches in the round on a needle. Transfer the remaining 15 stitches to holders in groups of 3.

*

1ST PETAL

Position the flower so the peduncle is facing you.

Row 1 (WS): P3.

Row 2 (RS): K1, M1-R, k1, M1-L, k1—5 stitches.

Row 3: P5.

Row 4: Kfb, M1-R, k3, M1-L, kfb—9 stitches.

Row 5: P9.

Row 6: K1, M1-R, knit to the last stitch, M1-L, k1—11 stitches.

Rows 7–13: Work in stockinette stitch.

Row 14: Ssk, knit to the last 2 stitches, k2tog—9 stitches.

Row 15: Purl.

Rows 16–19: Repeat rows 14 and 15 twice—5 stitches.

Row 20: Ssk, k1, k2tog—3 stitches.

Row 21: P3.

Row 22: Sk2p—1 stitch. Cut the yarn and draw the tail through the remaining stitch to finish off. Weave in the ends along the underside edges of the petal so that the petal tips appear rounded.

*

2ND–6TH PETALS

Transfer the 3 stitches to the left of the just-completed petal onto a double-pointed needle to work the next petal. Join a new strand of C and work as for the 1st petal.

——————— N O T E ———————

I recommend wiring the stem and petals. The flute does not require wiring.

Pom-Pom Chrysanthemum

Dendranthema morifolium

DIFFICULTY LEVEL 🖊 🖊 🖊

REQUIRED YARN COLORS

Green (A), white and/or pale pink (B), *Fizz* in yellow (C), and lighter-gauge yarn in yellow (D)

SAMPLE

Finished Measurements

Flower head diameter: 10" (25.5cm) unfelted

Peduncle length: 12" (30.5cm) or desired length

Yarns Used

Nashua Handknits *Creative Focus Bulky* New Fern #1265 (A) and Natural #0100 and Soft Pink #1837 (B)

Crystal Palace *Fizz* Lemonade #9221 (C)

Alpaca with a Twist *Fino* Yellow Ribbon #5010 (D)

PATTERN NOTES

- You will need a set of double-pointed and circular needles. I used size 13 (9mm) needles.
- Use a double strand of your chosen yarn.

PEDUNCLE
(MAIN STEM)

With A, cast on 5 stitches.

I-Cord Round: Knit across; without turning your work, slip the row to the other end of the needle; pull the yarn across the back to begin the next round.

Repeat the I-cord round for 72 rounds or desired length.

*

RECEPTACLE
(FLOWER FOUNDATION)

Divide the stitches onto 2 double-pointed needles.

Round 1: Kfb around—10 stitches.

Round 2: Kfb around—20 stitches.

Transfer every other stitch to 2 needles held to the center for the pistil; transfer the remaining 10 stitches to 5 holders (2 stitches on each) held to the outside for the sepal leaves. Cut the yarn and weave in the ends to secure.

*

PISTIL

Join single strands of B and C.

Rounds 1–5: With B and C held together, knit around. Cut the yarns and draw the ends through the remaining 10 stitches to finish off. Weave in the ends on the inside of the pistil.

1ST SEPAL LEAF

Position the flower so that the peduncle is facing you and the flower center is facing away from you.

Transfer 2 sepal stitches to a needle and join a new strand of A.

Row 1 (RS): Kfb, M1, kfb—5 stitches.

Rows 2–4: Work in stockinette stitch.

Row 5: Ssk, k1, k2tog—3 stitches.

Row 6: P3.

Row 7: Sk2p—1 stitch.

Cut the yarn and pull the tail through the remaining stitch to fasten off. Weave in the end on the wrong-side edge of the sepal leaf.

*

2ND–5TH SEPAL LEAVES

Transfer the 2 stitches to the left of the leaf just completed to a double-pointed needle to work the next leaf. Join A and work as for the 1st sepal leaf.

*

PETALS

With B and a circular needle, cast on 20 stitches.

Row 1 (WS): P20.

Row 2 (RS): Kfb in each stitch—40 stitches.

Rows 3–5: Work in stockinette stitch.

Row 6: *K1, kfb; repeat from * 20 times—60 stitches.

Rows 7–9: Work in stockinette stitch.

Row 10: Kfb in each stitch—120 stitches.

Bind-off Row: Using a cable cast-on method, cast on 13 stitches, bind off 14 stitches; *slip the remaining stitch

onto the left-hand needle, repeat from * until all stitches are bound off.

*

FINISHING

Starting at one end of the flower ruffle, with the right side facing out, coil the ruffle into a flower shape around the pistil, keeping the cast-on edge aligned.

Wrap the ruffle around the pistil until you have used the entire ruffle. Using a tapestry needle and a like-colored strand of yarn, sew the ruffle in place until secure, making sure to sew through all layers and all the way across the flower at the base and up to about 2" (5cm) from the base or cast-on edge.

Tack the sepal leaves to the underside of the flower.

*

STAMENS
(OPTIONAL)

Cut 15 strands of F, each 4" (10cm) long, adjusting the strand length for smaller- or larger-gauge flowers. Refer to the instructions on making stamens on page 30. Place the stamens in the center of the pistil. Trim the strands to approximately 1" (2.5cm) or an appropriately scaled length.

Purple
Shamrock
Oxalis triangularis

DIFFICULTY LEVEL 𝟢 𝟢 𝟢 𝟢

REQUIRED YARN COLORS
Light green (A) and white or pale
violet (B)

SAMPLE
Finished Measurements
Flower head diameter: 1½" (3.8cm)
Stem length: 6" (15cm)

Yarns Used
Stonehedge Fiber Mill *Shepherd's Wool*
(worsted weight) Spring Green (A)
and White (B)

PEDUNCLE (MAIN STEM)

With A, cast on 3 stitches.

I-Cord Round: Knit across; without turning your work, slip the row to the other end of the needle; pull the yarn across the back to begin the next round.

Repeat the I-cord round for 36 rounds or desired length.

*

RECEPTACLE (FLOWER FOUNDATION) & SETUP FOR PETAL BASE (COROLLA & CALYX)

Round 1: Kfb, k1, kfb—5 stitches.

Round 2: Join a new strand of A. With 2 strands of A held together, knit around.

Transfer every other A stitch to holders held to the outside to work the calyx later. Transfer the remaining stitches to 2 needles held to the center to work the corolla.

*

COROLLA

With A, work 2 rounds in the same manner as the peduncle; that is, in the round as an I-cord, but now work in reverse stockinette.

Round 3: P2, pfb, p1, pfb—7 stitches.

Rounds 4–8: Purl around.

Round 9: P3, pfb, p3—8 stitches.

Round 10: Change to B and purl around.

Round 11: Purl around.

Round 12: [P1, M1-P, p1] 4 times—12 stitches; W&T. Divide the stitches evenly among 3 needles. Position the flower so that the center is facing you and knit in the opposite direction of the previous round.

Round 13: [K2, M1, k2] 3 times—15 stitches.

Keep the 3 stitches worked first during the previous round on the needle; transfer the remaining 12 stitches to holders in groups of 3.

*

1ST PETAL

Row 1 (RS): K1, kfb, k1—4 stitches.

Row 2: P4.

Row 3: K2, M1, k2—5 stitches.

Rows 4–10: Work in stockinette stitch.

Row 11: Ssk, k1, k2tog and *at the same time* bind off.

Cut the yarn and fasten off. Weave in the end along the underside edge of the petal so that the petal tips appear rounded.

*

2ND–5TH PETALS

Transfer the 3 stitches to the left of the petal just completed to a needle. Join a new strand of B and work as for the 1st petal.

*

CALYX

Transfer the 5 A stitches to 2 needles. With the peduncle facing you, work in the round *around* the corolla of the flower.

Round 1: Kfb, k1, kfb, k1, kfb—8 stitches.

Round 2: Knit around.

Round 3: [K2, M1, k2] twice—10 stitches.

Rounds 4–10: Knit around.

Bind-off Round: Using the backwards-loop cast-on method (and still working in the round), *cast on 3 stitches; bind off 5 stitches; slip the remaining stitch from the right-hand needle onto the left-hand needle; repeat from * until all stitches are bound off.

Attach the first sepal leaf to the last as you weave in ends.

*

FINISHING

Tack the sepal leaf edges to the flower flute, if necessary, using invisible stitches.

Rose

Rosa multiflora

DIFFICULTY LEVEL ◊◊◊◊

REQUIRED YARN COLORS

Medium green (A) and crimson or the color of your choice (B)

SAMPLE

Finished Measurements

Flower head diameter: 3" (7.5cm)

Peduncle (main stem) length: 12" (30.5cm)

Yarns Used

Stonehedge Fiber Mill *Shepherd's Wool* (worsted weight) Lime (A)

Alpaca with a Twist *Baby Twist* Red Wagon #3007 (B)

PATTERN NOTE

When working across short rows, there's no need to hide the wraps.

INSTRUCTIONS

PEDUNCLE (MAIN STEM)

With A, cast on 3 stitches.

I-Cord Round: Knit across; without turning your work, slip the row to the other end of the needle; pull the yarn across the back to begin the next round.

Repeat the I-cord round for 48 rounds or desired length.

RECEPTACLE (FLOWER FOUNDATION)

Round 1: K1, M1, k1, M1, k1—5 stitches.

Round 2: Knit around.

Round 3: Kfb around—10 stitches.

Divide the stitches between 2 needles.

Rounds 4–7: Knit around.

Round 8: Ssk around—5 stitches.

Round 9: Knit.

Round 10: Kfb around—10 stitches.

Cut the yarn and weave in the ends. Transfer 8 stitches to 4 holders (2 stitches on each), leaving 2 stitches on the needle.

*

1ST SEPAL LEAF

Position the flower so that the peduncle is pointing down and away and the flower center is facing you.

Row 1 (RS): Join a strand of A; k1, M1, k1—3 stitches.

Row 2: P3.

Row 3: K3.

Row 4: P3.

Row 5: K1, k2tog—2 stitches.

Row 6: P2.

Row 7: K2tog—1 stitch.

Cut the yarn and draw the tail through the remaining stitch to fasten off. If felting, cut off the tail after felting. If leaving unfelted, weave the end in on the wrong-side edge of the sepal leaf.

*

2ND–5TH SEPAL LEAVES

Transfer the 2 stitches to the left of the leaf just completed to a needle.

Join a new strand of A and work as for the 1st sepal leaf.

*

BLOSSOM

The rose flower is made separately and then attached to the stem in the center of the sepal leaves.

Receptacle (flower foundation)

With a double-pointed needle and B, cast on 10 stitches.

Row 1 (RS): Kfb in each stitch—20 stitches.

Row 2: P20.

Row 3: Kfb in each stitch—40 stitches.

Row 4: P40.

1st Petal (centermost petal)

Row 1 (RS): [Kfb] twice, then transfer the remaining 38 stitches to a large holder for the outer petals—4 stitches.

Row 2: P4.

Row 3: K1, M1-R, k2, M1-L, k1—6 stitches.

Rows 4–8: Work in stockinette stitch.

Row 9 (short row): K4, W&T.

Row 10 (short row): P2, W&T.

Row 11: K4.

Row 12: P2tog, p2, ssp—4 stitches.

Bind off purlwise on the right side.

Cut the yarn and weave in the end.

2nd Petal

With the right side facing you, transfer the next 2 stitches to a needle and join a new strand of B. Work as for the 1st petal.

3rd–8th Petals

With the right side again facing you,

transfer the next 2 stitches to a needle and join a new strand of B.

Row 1 (RS): Kfbf in each stitch— 6 stitches.

Row 2: P6.

Row 3: K1, M1-R, k4, M1-L, k1—8 stitches.

Rows 4–6: Work in stockinette stitch.

Row 7 (short row): K6, W&T.

Row 8 (short row): P4, W&T.

Row 9 (short row): K3, W&T.

Row 10 (short row): P2, W&T.

Row 11 (short row): K5.

Bind off knitwise on the wrong side. Cut the yarn and weave in the ends at the base and apex of the petal.

9th–14th Petals

With the right side facing you, transfer the next 4 stitches to a needle and join a new strand of B.

Row 1 (RS): Kfb in each stitch—8 stitches.

Row 2: P8.

Row 3: Kfb, k6, kfb—10 stitches.

Rows 4–8: Work in stockinette stitch.

Row 9 (short row): K7, W&T.

Row 10 (short row): P4, W&T.

Row 11 (short row): K3, W&T.

Row 12 (short row): P2, W&T.

Row 13 (short row): K6.

Bind off knitwise on the wrong side. Cut the yarn and weave in the ends at the base and apex of the petal along the wrong-side edge.

*

FINISHING

With the right (knit) side facing out, allow the work to spiral around the 2 smallest petals. It's important to keep the cast-on edge at the same level. It may be easiest to sew the petals in place as they spiral, using a darning needle and a strand of the same yarn. Use a darning needle and like-colored yarn to sew first through the cast-on edge, going through all thicknesses. Then sew through the entire diameter of the flower, beginning at the flower base and ending up about 1" (2.5cm) from the flower base. Put the needle back in about where you came out, going directly across the flower 1" (2.5cm), or an appropriately scaled distance, from the base. Don't pull too tight, as that will pull the petals in too far. The objective here is for the flower to appear to be opening but not so much that it looks as though it's falling apart. If the securing stitches are too low, the flower will begin to droop; if too high, it will appear to be too tight or not yet unfurled. You may want to play with these differences, creating roses that are at different stages of unfurling. Once the flower has been assembled, secure the blossom in the center of the sepal leaves with a darning needle and like-colored yarn or a sewing needle and a double strand of sewing thread and invisible stitches.

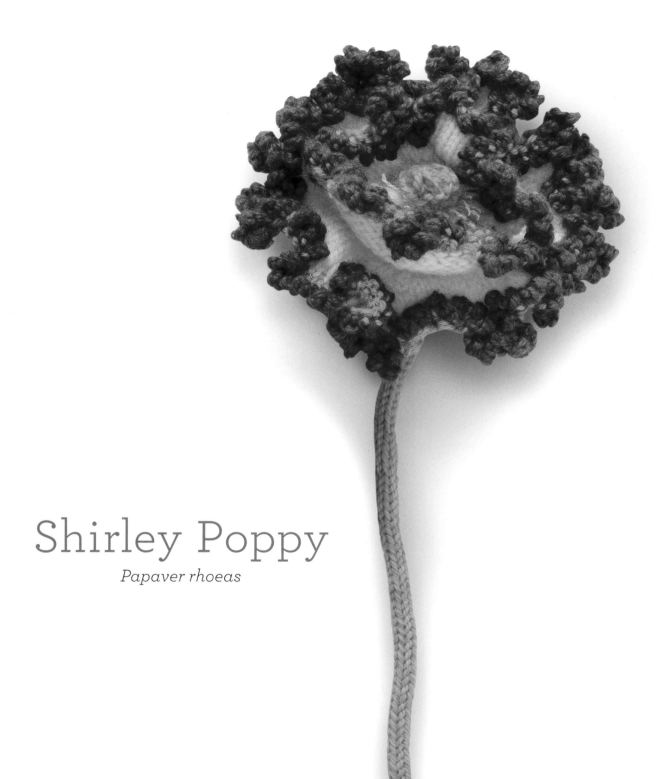

Shirley Poppy
Papaver rhoeas

REQUIRED YARN COLORS

Light green (A), white (B), medium
pink (C), red (D), and lighter-gauge
yellow (E)

SAMPLE

Finished Measurements
Flower blossom diameter: 5" (12.5cm)
Stem length: 12" (30.5cm)

Yarns Used
Stonehedge Fiber Mill *Shepherd's Wool*
(worsted weight) Spring Green (A),
White (B), Zinnia Pink (C), Christmas
Red (D), and (fingering weight)
Spring Chick (E)

PATTERN NOTE

When working across short rows,
there's no need to hide the wraps.

INSTRUCTIONS

PEDUNCLE (MAIN STEM)

With A, cast on 4 stitches.

I-Cord Round: Knit across; without
turning your work, slip the row to the
other end of the needle; pull the yarn
across the back to begin the next
round.

Repeat the I-cord round for 72 rounds
or desired length.

PISTIL

Round 1: Kfb in each stitch—8
stitches.

Divide the stitches between 2 needles.

Round 2: Join a strand of B; with A
and B held together, knit around.
Transfer the 8 A stitches to 2 needles
and hold in the center to continue
to make the pistil; transfer the 8 B
stitches to 4 holders (2 stitches each)
held to the outside for the petals. Cut
the strand of B, tie the B ends together
in a square knot and weave in the
ends within the same color field.
Divide the stitches between 2 needles.

Round 3: With A, knit around.

Round 4: [K1, M1, k1] 4 times—12
stitches.

Round 5: Knit around.

Round 6: Purl around.

Round 7: Knit around.

Round 8: [K2tog] 6 times—6 stitches.
Cut the yarn and pull through the
remaining 6 stitches. Weave the end
into the pistil center to secure.

*

1ST SMALL PETAL

Position the flower so that the pistil is
facing up toward you and the stem is
facing down.

Transfer 2 B stitches to a needle. Join
a new strand of B.

Row 1 (RS): Kfbf in each stitch—6
stitches.

Row 2: P6.

Row 3: Kfb in each stitch—12 stitches.

Row 4: Purl across.

Row 5: [Kfb] twice, k8, [kfb] twice—
16 stitches.

Row 6: P16.

Row 7: Kfb, k to the last stitch,
kfb—18 stitches.

Row 8 (short row): P15, W&T.

Row 9 (short row): K12, W&T.

Row 10 (short row): P9, W&T.

Row 11 (short row): K6, W&T.

Row 12 (short row): P5, W&T.

Row 13 (short row): K4, W&T.

Row 14 (short row): P11.

Row 15: Knit all stitches.

Row 16: Purl all stitches.

Row 17 (short row): K12, W&T.

Row 18 (short row): P6, W&T.

Row 19 (short row): K5, W&T.

Row 20 (short row): P4, W&T.

Row 21: K11.

Row 22: Change to C and purl
across.

Row 23: [Kfb, kfbf] 9 times—45
stitches.

Row 24: Purl all stitches.

Picot Bind-off: Change to D and
using a cable cast-on, *cast on 2
stitches, then bind off 3 stitches;
repeat from * until all stitches are
bound off. Cut the yarn and weave
in the ends along same-color-field
edges so that the tips of the picot
bind-off are tacked to the edge of
the petal. This way, the ruffled edge
appears to extend down the petal
edge.

*

2ND SMALL PETAL

Transfer the 2 stitches directly opposite the 1st small petal to a needle
(there should be 2 stitches on hold
between each of the 2 small petals;
that is, the stitches for the large petals
are located between the small petals

and are opposite each other). Join a new strand of B and work the 2nd small flower petal as for the 1st.

*

1ST LARGE PETAL

Transfer 2 stitches between the small petals to a needle.

Row 1 (RS): Join a new strand of B; kfbf in each stitch—6 stitches.

Row 2: Purl across.

Row 3: Kfbf, [kfb] 4 times, kfbf—14 stitches.

Row 4: Purl across.

Row 5: [Kfb] twice, knit to the last 2 stitches, [kfb] twice—18 stitches.

Row 6: Purl across.

Row 7: Kfb, knit to the last stitch, kfb—20 stitches.

Row 8: Purl across.

Row 9: Kfb, knit to the last stitch, kfb—22 stitches.

Row 10: Purl across.

Rows 11–14: Repeat rows 7 and 8 twice—26 stitches.

Row 15: K8, [kfb] 10 times, k8—36

stitches.

Row 16 (short row): P30, W&T.

Row 17 (short row): K24, W&T.

Row 18 (short row): P18, W&T.

Row 19 (short row): K12, W&T.

Row 20: Purl to the end.

Row 21: Knit all stitches.

Row 22: Change to C and purl across.

Row 23: [Kfb, kfbf] 18 times—90 stitches.

Row 24: Purl across.

Picot Bind-off: Change to D and using a cable cast-on, *cast on 2 stitches, then bind off 3 stitches; repeat from * until all stitches are bound off. Cut the yarn and weave in the ends along the same-color-field edge as for the small petals.

*

2ND LARGE PETAL

Transfer the remaining 2 stitches to a needle.

Work the 2nd large flower petal as for the 1st.

FLOWER ASSEMBLY

Tack the small petals to each other at their base and their tips. Tack the large petals to each other at their base, and then begin to tack them together again about halfway to just a bit before the outermost edge. Use images of actual Shirley poppies to guide your efforts.

*

STAMENS

If felting, create stamens *after* felting is complete. Cut 15 strands of E (or sufficient strands to surround the pistil), each 3" (7.5cm) long. Adjust the strand length for smaller- or larger-gauge flowers. Refer to the instructions for making stamens on page 30. Once stamens are complete, trim the strands to approximately ½" (13mm) or flush with the top of the pistil.

Star Magnolia

Magnolia stellata

DIFFICULTY LEVEL ◊ ◊ ◊ ◊

REQUIRED YARN COLORS
Twig brown (A), white (B), and
lighter-gauge yarn in pale pink (C)

SAMPLE
Finished Measurements
Flower head diameter: 6" (15cm)
Twig length: 4" (10cm)

Yarns Used
Stonehedge Fiber Mill *Shepherd's Wool*
(worsted weight) Milk Chocolate (A),
White (B), and (fingering weight)
Baby Pink (C)

PATTERN NOTES
- You will need a set of needles
  approximately 5 sizes smaller for
  the stamens.
- When working across short rows,
  there's no need to hide the wraps.

PEDUNCLE
(MAIN STEM)

With A, cast on 3 stitches.
I-Cord Round: Knit across; without
turning your work, slip the row to the
other end of the needle; pull the yarn
across the back to begin the next
round.
Repeat the I-cord round for 24 rounds
or desired length.
Round 1: K1, M1, k1, M1, k1—5
stitches.
Round 2: Knit around.
Round 3: Kfb in each stitch—10
stitches.
Divide the stitches between 2 needles.

*

RECEPTACLE
(FLOWER FOUNDATION)

Round 1: Join a strand of B and a
strand of C; with A, B, and C held
together, knit around.
Transfer the A stitches to 3 holders as
follows: the first A stitch to a holder
held to the center for the pistil, the
next 4 A stitches to a holder held to
the outside for a sepal leaf, the next A
stitch to the pistil holder, and the last
4 A stitches to a holder held to the
outside for a 2nd sepal leaf.
Transfer the B stitches to 2 holders for
petals (5 stitches each), held just inside
the sepal stitches. Transfer the C stitches
to 2 holders for stamens (5 stitches
each), held between the pistil (A)
stitches and the petal (B) stitches. Keep
A live to work the pistil. Cut the strands
of B and C, tie the ends together, and

weave in B ends on the underside
edges of the petals and the C ends
into the stamens once they are made.

*

SEPAL LEAVES

With the peduncle facing you and the
flower center facing away, transfer
1 group of 4 A sepal stitches to a
needle.
Row 1 (RS): Join a new strand of A;
kfb, M1-R, k2, M1-L, kfb—8 stitches.
Row 2: P8.
Row 3 (short row): K6, W&T.
Row 4 (short row): P4, W&T.
Row 5 (short row): K3, W&T.
Row 6 (short row): P2, W&T.
Row 7 (short row): K1, W&T.
Row 8: P4.
Rows 9–12: Work across all stitches
in stockinette stitch.
Row 13: Ssk, k4, k2tog—6 stitches.
Row 14: P2tog, p2, ssp—4 stitches.
Row 15: Ssk, k2tog—2 stitches.
Row 16: P2.
Cut the yarn and draw the tail
through the remaining 2 stitches to
fasten off.
Weave in the end along the wrong
side of the sepal leaf base and edge.
Work the 2nd sepal leaf as for the 1st.

*

PISTIL

Transfer the 2 A stitches held in the
center to a needle.
With the live strand of A, knit 4 I-cord
rounds.
Cut the yarn and pull the tail through
the last 2 stitches to fasten off.

Weave in the ends into the center of the pistil.

*

STAMENS

Transfer the 10 C stitches to 2 smaller-gauge parallel needles.

Round 1: Join a strand of C; kfb in each stitch—20 stitches.

Transfer the stitches to needles/holders as follows: Put every other stitch on a size 1 needle held to the center, and put the remaining 10 stitches on 2 or more holders held to the outside of these center stitches.

Bind-off Row (RS): With the live strand of C and the stitches on the needle, use the backwards-loop cast-on method to *cast on 6 stitches, bind off 7 stitches, slip the remaining stitch from the right- to the left-hand needle; repeat from * until all 10 stitches have been bound off.

Transfer the remaining 10 C stitches to 2 or more needles.

Bind-off Row (RS): Join a new strand of C; using the backwards-loop cast-on method, *cast on 5 stitches, bind off 6 stitches; slip the remaining stitch from the right- to the left-hand needle repeat from * until all 10 stitches have been bound off.

Cut the yarn and pull the tail through the last stitch to finish off.

Weave in the ends around the pistil to tighten up the center.

*

RECEPTACLE (CONTINUED)

With the flower center facing you, transfer the 10 B stitches to 2 needles.

Round 2: Join a double strand of B and knit around—20 single-strand stitches.

Starting at the beginning of the round, *transfer the 1st single-strand stitch to a holder held to the center, transfer the next single-strand stitch to a needle held to the outside; repeat from * 4 more times, ending with 5 stitches on the holder and 5 stitches on a needle. Repeat once more using a new holder and needle—10 stitches on 2 holders in the center and 10 stitches on 2 needles held to the outside.

*

OUTER PETALS

Position the flower so that the peduncle is facing away and the flower center is facing you.

Round 1: With the live strand of B attached to the outside stitches, kfb around—20 stitches.

Keep the first 2 stitches of the round on a needle to work the 1st petal, putting the remaining 18 stitches on 9 holders (2 stitches on each).

1st Outer Petal

Row 1 (RS): With live strand of B; k1, Ll-R, k1—3 stitches.

Row 2: P3.

Row 3: K1, M1-R, k1, M1-L, k1—5 stitches.

Rows 4–26: Work in stockinette stitch.

Row 27: Ssk, k1, k2tog—3 stitches. Bind off.

Weave the end in along the petal underside edge so that the petal tip appears blunt and rounded.

2nd–10th Outer Petals

Transfer the 2 stitches to the left of the petal just completed to a needle. Join a strand of B and complete as for the 1st petal.

*

INNER PETALS

Transfer the center 10 B stitches to 2 needles. Position the flower so the center is facing you.

Round 1: With the second live strand of B attached to the inner petals, kfb around, then knit the 1st stitch of the next round—20 stitches.

Keep the first 2 stitches to the left of the live yarn on a needle to work the 1st petal, putting the remaining 18 stitches on 9 holders (2 stitches on each). Work the 10 inner petals as for the outer petals.

— NOTE —

Magnolia flower petals benefit greatly from wiring.

Sunflower

Helianthus annuus

REQUIRED YARN COLORS

Green (A), brown (B), and red, orange, or yellow (C), and a short length of Crystal Palace *Fizz* in brown (D)

SAMPLE

Finished Measurements
Flower head diameter: varies with gauge
Stem length: varies with gauge

Yarns Used
Flower 1 (opposite, bottom left): Plymouth *Galway* and *Galway Highland Heather* Turtle Heather #754 (A), Bark Heather #757 (B), Lemon Zest #179 (C), and Crystal Palace *Fizz* Mink #7342 (D)
Flower 2 (opposite, top left): Plymouth *Galway* and *Galway Highland Heather* Turtle Heather Turtle Heather #754 (A), Bark Heather #757 (B), Clementine Orange #91 (C), and Crystal Palace *Fizz* Mink #7342 (D)
Flower 3 (opposite, top right): Plymouth *Galway* and *Galway Highland Heather* Turtle Heather Apple Green #127 (A), Bark Heather #757 (B), Apricot #154 (C), and Crystal Palace *Fizz* Mink #7342 (D)
Flower 4 (opposite, bottom right): Plymouth *Galway* and *Galway Highland Heather* Turtle Heather Turtle Heather #754 (A), Bark Heather #757 (B), Apricot #154 (C), and Crystal Palace *Fizz* Mink #7342 (D)
Flower 5 (opposite, bottom center): Plymouth *Galway* and *Galway Highland Heather* Turtle Heather Apple Green #127 (A), Bark Heather #757

(B), Golden Heather #755 (C), and Crystal Palace *Fizz* Mink #7342 (D)

PATTERN NOTE

You may wish to use circular needles for ease of working.

INSTRUCTIONS

PEDUNCLE
(MAIN STEM)

With A and a double-pointed needle, cast on 8 stitches. Divide between 2 needles and fold so that wrong sides are facing each other (see page 24 for Working in the Round: I-Cord Stems of Different Sizes). Work in the round for 180 rounds or desired length.

*

RECEPTACLE

Round 1: Kfb in each stitch around—16 stitches.
Divide evenly among 4 double-pointed needles and mark the beginning of the round.
Round 2: Knit.
Round 3: *K2, M1, k2; repeat from * around—20 stitches.
Rounds 4 and 5: Knit.
Round 6: *K2, M1, k2, M1, k1; repeat from * around—28 stitches.
Round 7: Knit.
Round 8: *K1, M1, k2, M1, k1, M1, k2, M1, k1; repeat from * around—44 stitches.
Round 9: Knit.

Round 10: *K2, M1, k2, M1, k1, kfb, k1, M1, k2, M1, k2; repeat from * around—64 stitches.
Round 11: Knit.
Round 12: Holding A, B, and C together, knit the 3 colors into each stitch. It will make it easier to do the next step if you keep these colored stitches in the same order and do not let them twist around each other as you knit. It also may be easier to work this step using a 16" (40.5cm) circular needle.
Move the stitches for each color onto separate holders using strands of scrap yarn or spare circular needles. Position the colors as follows: Put all B stitches on 1 holder held toward the center, all C stitches on another holder between B and A stitches, and all A stitches on a holder held to the outside. Do not cut the yarns.

*

FLOWER CENTER

Slip all B stitches onto 4 double-pointed needles (16 stitches each needle) or 1 circular needle (64 stitches total); place a marker and join.
With flower center facing you, join D, hold together with the live strand of B and work as follows:
Round 1: Purl around.
Round 2: *[P1, p2tog] twice, p4, [p2tog, p1] twice; repeat from * around—48 stitches.
Round 3: Purl.
Round 4: *P2, p2tog, p4, p2tog, p2; repeat from * around—40 stitches.
Round 5: Purl.
Round 6: *[P2, p2tog] twice, p2;

repeat from * around—32 stitches.

Round 7: Purl.

Round 8: *P1, p2tog, p2, p2tog, p1;
repeat from * around—24 stitches.

Round 9: *P2, p2tog, p2; repeat from
* around—20 stitches.

Round 10: *P1, p2tog, p2; repeat
from * around—16 stitches.

Round 11: *P1, p2tog, p1; repeat
from * around—12 stitches.

Round 12: *P2tog, p1; repeat from *
around—8 stitches.

Cut the yarn and pull the end through
the remaining 8 stitches. Weave the
end to the inside to secure.

*

SEPAL LEAVES

With the peduncle facing you, *slip
the 4 A stitches immediately to the
left of the live strand of A onto a
double-pointed needle or working
circular needle and work the stitches
as follows:

Row 1: K4.

Row 2: P4.

Row 3: Ssk, k2tog—2 stitches.

Row 4: P2tog—1 stitch.

Cut the yarn, leaving a 4" (10cm) tail,
and draw the tail through the stitch
to finish off. Weave in the end on the
wrong-side edge of the sepal.

Rejoin A and repeat from * until all
the A stitches have been worked.

PETALS

Slip all C stitches onto 3 double-
pointed or a single 16" (40.5cm)
circular needle.

*Use the backwards-loop cast-on
method to cast 9 stitches onto the left-
hand needle.

Bind off 9 cast-on stitches—1 stitch
remains on the right-hand needle.

Slip 1 stitch onto the right needle and
bind off the 1st stitch by passing it
over the slipped stitch.

Slip the remaining stitch back onto the
left needle. Repeat from * until all 64
stitches are bound off, then fasten off
the last stitch and weave in the end.

Sweetheart Rose

Rosa polyantha

DIFFICULTY LEVEL 🌿🌿🌿

REQUIRED YARN COLORS
Moss or lime green (A) and pink or red (B)

SAMPLE
Finished Measurements
Flower bud height: 2" (5cm)
Stem length: 6" (15cm)

Yarns Used
Alpaca with a Twist *Baby Twist* Alfalfa #4004 (A) and Red Wagon #3007 (B)

PATTERN NOTE
When working across short rows, there's no need to hide the wraps.

INSTRUCTIONS

PEDUNCLE (MAIN STEM)
With A, cast on 3 stitches.
I-Cord Round: Knit across; without turning your work, slip the row to the other end of the needle; pull the yarn across the back to begin the next round.
Repeat the I-cord round for 36 rounds or desired length.

RECEPTACLE (FLOWER FOUNDATION)

Round 1: K1, M1, k1, M1, k1—5 stitches.

Round 2: Knit around.

Round 3: Kfb around—10 stitches. Divide stitches between 2 needles.

Rounds 4–7: Knit around.

Round 8: Ssk around—5 stitches. Keep on 2 needles or consolidate to a single needle.

Round 9: Knit.

Round 10: Kfb around. Divide between 2 needles—10 stitches.

Round 11: [K1, then place 1 stitch (unworked) on a holder held to the outside] 5 times—5 worked stitches on 1 needle for the rosebud, 5 unworked stitches on 2–3 holders to the outside for the sepals. Do not cut A.

✳

ROSEBUD

Round 1: Change to a double strand of B and knit around.

[K1, then place 1 stitch (unworked) on a holder held to the outside] 5 times—5 worked stitches on 1 needle for the center rosebud, 5 unworked stitches on 2–3 holders to the outside for unfurling rose petals.

Round 2: With a single live strand of B, k2, M1, k3—6 stitches.

Round 3: Kfb around—12 stitches.

Rounds 4–7: Knit.

Round 8: [Ssk, k2, k2tog] twice—8 stitches.

Round 9: Knit.

Round 10: [Ssk, k2tog] twice—4 stitches.

Round 11: Knit.

Rounds 12 and 13: Knit.

Cut the yarn; pull the tail end through the remaining 4 stitches. Weave in the end to the inside of the bud.

✳

PETALS

Transfer the 5 B stitches to 2 needles. Position the flower so that the rosebud is facing away from you and the peduncle is between you and the rosebud.

Round 1: With the 2nd live strand of B, k2, kfb, k2—6 stitches. Keep the first 2 stitches in the round on a needle. Transfer the remaining 4 stitches to holders in groups of 2.

Row 1 (RS): Kfbf in each stitch—6 stitches.

Row 2: P6.

Row 3: K1, M1-R, k4, M1-L, k1—8 stitches.

Rows 4–6: Work in stockinette stitch.

Row 7 (short row): K6, W&T.

Row 8 (short row): P4, W&T.

Row 9 (short row): K3, W&T.

Row 10 (short row): P2, W&T.

Row 11 (short row): K5.

Row 12: P2tog, p4, ssp—6 stitches.

Row 13: Ssk, k2, k2tog—4 stitches. Bind off knitwise on the wrong side. Cut the yarn and weave in the ends on the underside edges of the petals.

✳

SEPAL LEAVES

Transfer the 5 A stitches to 2 needles. Position the flower so that the rosebud is facing away from you and the peduncle is between you and the rosebud.

Round 1: With the live strand of A, kfb in each stitch—10 stitches.

Round 2: Knit around. Keep the first 2 stitches of the round on a needle. Transfer the remaining 8 stitches to holders in groups of 2.

✳

1ST SEPAL LEAF

Continue with the flower positioned as above, with the rosebud facing away from you and the peduncle between you and the rosebud.

Row 1 (RS): K1, M1, k1—3 stitches.

Rows 2–6: Work in stockinette stitch.

Row 7: K1, k2tog—2 stitches.

Rows 8–10: Work in stockinette stitch.

Row 11: K2tog—1 stitch.

Cut the yarn and draw the tail through the remaining stitch to fasten off. Use the tails to tack the sepal leaves to the rose blossom as desired. Weave in the remaining ends on the sepal leaf wrong-side edges.

✳

2ND–5TH SEPAL LEAVES

Transfer the 2 stitches to the left of the leaf just completed to a needle. Join a new strand of A and work as for the 1st sepal leaf.

✳

FINISHING

Allow the tips of the rose petals to curl outward at the top. Tack the rose petals to the rosebud using like-colored yarn or sewing thread and a sharp needle. Tack the sepal leaves to the outside of the rose flower or leave them curled downward as desired.

Tulip

Tulipa hybrida

DIFFICULTY LEVEL 🖋🖋🖋🖋

REQUIRED YARN COLORS

Medium green (A); yellow, very dark purple, or black (B); red, bright pink, bright orange, or the color of your choice (C); lighter-gauge yarn in pale yellow, green, or white (D); and yellow or very dark purple (E).

SAMPLE

Finished Measurements
Flower head diameter: 9" (23cm)
Stem length: 18" (45.5cm)

Yarns Used
Stonehedge Fiber Mill *Shepherd's Wool* (worsted weight) Lime Green (A), Spring Chick (B), Antique Rose (C) and (fingering weight) Spring Green (D) and Spring Chick (E)

PATTERN NOTES

- I encourage you to look at tulips closely and to choose colors that match the exuberance and variety of real tulips—the options are endless and inspiring. Any single suggested palette is limiting.
- The color changes in the petals should be worked as intarsia; use separate strands of yarn for the different colors. Interlock the yarns at the color changes to prevent holes.
- You will need a set of needles approximately 5 sizes smaller for the stamens.
- When working across short rows, there's no need to hide the wraps.

PEDUNCLE
(MAIN STEM)

With A, cast on 4 stitches.
I-Cord Round: Knit across; without turning your work, slip the row to the other end of the needle; pull the yarn across the back to begin the next round.
Repeat the I-cord round for 110 rounds or desired length.

*

RECEPTACLE
(FLOWER FOUNDATION)

Round 1: [Kfb] 3 times, kfbf—9 stitches.
Divide stitches between 2 needles. Cut A, leaving a long tail and weave the end in down the center of the peduncle.
Round 2: With a double strand of B, knit around—9 double stitches. Transfer every other of the B stitches to 3 needles (in groups of 3) held to the outside for petals. Of the remaining 9 B stitches, transfer the 1st, 5th, and 9th stitches to a holder held to the center to work the pistil. Transfer the remaining 6 B stitches to needles held between the center B stitches and the outer B stitches for stamens.
Round 3: Return to the 9 petal stitches on 3 needles. With the live strand of B, purl around, W&T.
Round 4: You are now working in the opposite direction and the RS is the "inside": Kfb in each stitch—18 stitches.
Keep the first 3 stitches of the round

on a needle. Transfer the last 15 stitches to 5 holders (3 stitches on each).

*

1ST PETAL

This flower has been worked so that it will be displayed "open." To do this, orient the piece so that the pistil is facing you and the peduncle is facing away. This puts the right side of the flower on the inside.
Row 1: Kfb, k1, kfb—5 stitches.
Row 2: P5.
Row 3: Kfb, knit to the last stitch, kfb—7 stitches.
Row 4: P7.
Row 5: Repeat row 3—9 stitches.
Row 6: P9. Cut B and weave in the end on the underside edge of the petal.
Row 7: Join a strand of C; k1, M1-R, k2, join a new strand of B and k3, join a new strand of C and k2, M1-L, k1—11 stitches. *Note:* At color intersections, be sure to cross your yarns so that you don't end up with holes in your work.
Row 8: C: P4; B: p3; C: P4.
Row 9: C: K1, M1-R, k4; B: K1; C: K4, M1-L, k1—13 stitches.
Row 10: Purl in established color pattern. Cut B and weave in the end on the underside edge of the like-color field.
Row 11: With C, repeat row 3—15 stitches.
Row 12 (short row): P10, W&T.
Row 13 (short row): K5, W&T.
Row 14: P10.
Row 15: Repeat row 3—17 stitches.

Row 16: P17.

Row 17: Repeat row 3—19 stitches.

Rows 18–28: Work in stockinette stitch.

Row 29: K1, ssk, knit to the last 3 stitches, k2tog, k1—17 stitches.

Row 30: P1, p2tog, purl to the last 3 stitches, ssp, p1—15 stitches.

Rows 31–35: Repeat rows 29 and 30 until 5 stitches remain.

Row 36: P2tog, p1, ssp and *at the same time* bind off.

Cut the yarn and weave in the ends at the apex and base of the petal along petal edges.

✳

2ND–6TH PETALS

Transfer the 3 stitches to the left of the petal just completed to a needle. Join a new strand of B and work as for the 1st petal.

✳

PISTIL
Style

Transfer the 3 center B stitches to a double-pointed needle. Join a new strand of B and work the 3 center stitches as follows.

Round 1: Knit around.

Round 2: K1, kfb, k1—4 stitches.

Rounds 3–12: Knit around.

Round 13: K1, ssk, k1—3 stitches.

Stigma

*Use the backwards-loop cast-on method to cast on 3 stitches, then bind off 4 stitches; slip the remaining stitch onto the left-hand needle

and repeat from * until the 3 center stitches are bound off. Cut A and then weave the end into the center of the pistil so that the 1st and 3rd nodes of the stigma sit snugly next to each other.

✳

STAMENS

Transfer the 6 B stitches to 2 smaller-gauge double-pointed needles. Join a strand of E.

Round 1: Kfb in each stitch—12 stitches.

Round 2: Knit around. Keep the last 2 stitches worked on a needle and transfer the remaining 10 stitches to holders in groups of 2 or more.

1st Filament

Knit the 2 stitches as an I-cord for 13 rounds.

Next round: K2tog—1 stitch.

Anther

Using the backwards-loop cast-on method, cast on 8 stitches. Bind off the stitches. Cut the yarn. Weave in the end so as to tack the anther against the filament in such a way that the anther aligns itself vertically with its filament and faces away from the pistil.

2nd–6th Filaments

Transfer the 2 stitches to the left of the filament just completed to a smaller needle. Join a new strand of D and work as for the 1st filament and anther.

FINISHING

Arrange the petals so that 3 petals are brought to the fore, while 3 petals are somewhat recessed. Use like-colored sewing thread and a sharp needle to tack petals together. If you are wiring the petals, tack them together after completing the wiring process.

Wood Violet

Viola papilionacea

DIFFICULTY LEVEL 🖋🖋🖋🖋

REQUIRED YARN COLORS

Light or medium green (A) and white or purple (B)

SAMPLE

Finished Measurements
Flower blossom diameter: 2" (5cm)
Stem length: 4" (10cm)

Yarns Used
Stonehedge Fiber Mill *Shepherd's Wool* (fingering weight) Spring Green (A) and Lilac (B)

INSTRUCTIONS

PEDUNCLE
(MAIN STEM)

With A, cast on 3 stitches.

I-Cord Round: Knit across; without turning your work, slip the row to the other end of the needle; pull the yarn across the back to begin the next round.

Repeat the I-cord round for 24 rounds or desired length.

*

RECEPTACLE
(FLOWER FOUNDATION)

Round 1: Kfb in each stitch—6 stitches.

Divide the stitches between 2 needles.

Round 2: Change to B; knit around.

Round 3: K2, M1, k2, M1, k2—8 stitches.

Round 4: Kfb in each stitch—16 stitches.

PETALS

With the peduncle of the flower pointing down and what will become the flower center facing up and toward you, keep the last 6 stitches worked on a needle and transfer the remaining 10 stitches to holders.

1st Large Upper Petal

Row 1 (RS): You are now looking into the flower center and the stitches on holders should be closest to you, with the stitches on the needle in your left hand and the live yarn on the right end of the needle. With B you are now going to knit on what was formerly the wrong side. [K1, transfer 1 stitch (unworked) to a holder held to the back] 3 times—3 stitches on a needle in front; 3 stitches unworked on a holder in back for the 2nd large upper petal.

Row 2: P3.

Row 3: K1, M1-R, k1, M1-L, k1—5 stitches.

Row 4: P5.

Row 5: Kfb, k3, kfb—7 stitches.

Rows 6–10: Work in stockinette stitch.

Row 11: Ssk, knit to the last 2 stitches, k2tog—5 stitches.

Row 12: P5.

Row 13: Repeat row 11—3 stitches.
Bind off the remaining 3 stitches, cut yarn, and weave in the ends at the petal base and apex along the petal underside edges.

2nd Large Upper Petal

Transfer the 3 stitches held in back to a needle; position the flower so that the completed petal is on top and held forward. The petal center will

again be located between you and the petal you will now create.

Row 1 (RS): Join a new strand of B; k3.

Rows 2–13: Work as for the 1st petal.

*

TWO SMALL SIDE PETALS

Transfer the 2 stitches on either side of the large petals to 1 needle—4 stitches. Make sure the stitches are not twisted and position the flower center to face you.

Using B, knit 1 row and purl 1 row, making sure your stitches are quite snug in order to prevent the 2 small side petals from pulling apart in the flower center.

Keep the first 2 stitches on the needle for the 1st small side petal; transfer the last 2 stitches to a holder for the 2nd small side petal.

1st Side Petal

Row 1 (RS): K1, M1, k1—3 stitches.

Row 2: P3.

Row 3: K1, M1-R, k1, M1-L, k1—5 stitches.

Rows 4–8: Work in stockinette stitch.

Row 9: Ssk, k1, k2tog—3 stitches.

Row 10: P3.

Row 11: Sk2p—1 stitch.

Cut the yarn and pull the tail through the last stitch to fasten off. Weave in the ends.

2nd Side Petal

Transfer the 2 stitches on hold to a needle.

Join a new strand of B and work as for the 1st side petal.

SINGLE LOWER PETAL

Transfer the last 6 stitches to a needle. Keep the flower positioned so that the center is facing you.

Row 1 (RS): Join a new strand of B; k6.

Rows 2–8: Work in stockinette stitch.

Row 9: Ssk, k2, k2tog—4 stitches.

Row 10: P2tog, ssp—2 stitches.

Bind off.

Cut the yarn and weave in the ends.

FINISHING

If desired, use a tapestry needle and like-colored yarn to tack the 2 upper petals together so that they over-lap slightly in the center. Tack the 2 smaller side petals so that they incline to the left and right, respectively.

—————— TIP ——————

For a lovely gift bouquet of violets, make 7–9 violets and then tie them together with a ribbon.

Ylang-Ylang

Cananga odorata

REQUIRED YARN COLORS

Lime green (A), saffron yellow (B), and yellow-green (C)

SAMPLE

Finished Measurements

Flower head diameter from petal tip to petal tip: 9" (23cm)

Stem length: 4" (10cm)

Yarns Used

Stonehedge Fiber Mill *Shepherd's Wool* (worsted weight) Lime (A) and Lemon Yellow (B)

Tilli Tomas *Flurries* Saffron (C)

INSTRUCTIONS

PEDUNCLE
(MAIN STEM)

With A, cast on 2 stitches.

I-Cord Round: Knit across; without turning your work, slip the row to the other end of the needle; pull the yarn across the back to begin the next round. Mark the beginning of the round with a marker.

Repeat the I-cord round for 24 rounds or desired length.

*

RECEPTACLE
(FLOWER FOUNDATION)

Round 1: [Kfbf] twice—6 stitches. Divide the stitches between 2 needles.

Round 2: Knit around.

Round 3: Kfb in each stitch—12 stitches.

Round 4: Join a strand of B and a strand of C; holding A, B, and C together, knit around.

Transfer the 12 A stitches to 3 holders (4 stitches on each) held to the outside for the sepal leaves; transfer the 12 B stitches to 2 or more holders held just above the A stitches for petals; slip the 12 C stitches onto 2 parallel needles held to the center to work the pistil.

Cut A and weave in the end.

*

PISTIL

Position the flower so that the peduncle is facing you.

Round 1: Using the live strand of C, k2tog around—6 stitches.

Cut the yarn and pull the tail through the remaining 6 stitches; pull tight—the pistil will look like a little tiny pillow in the center of the flower.

Weave the end down into the center to secure.

*

1ST SEPAL LEAF

Position the flower so that the peduncle is facing you; that is, the stem is between you and the flower center. The 1st round establishes the wrong side of the sepal leaf as facing the stem with the right side facing the flower center and eventually the underside of the flower petals.

Transfer 4 A stitches to a needle. Join a new strand of A.

Row 1 (WS): P4.

Rows 2 and 3: Work in stockinette stitch.

Row 4: K1, ssk, k1—3 stitches.

Row 5: S1, ssp, psso—1 stitch.

Cut the yarn and pull the tail through the remaining stitch to fasten off. Weave in the ends at the apex and base of the sepal leaf along the underside edge of the leaf.

*

2ND–4TH SEPAL LEAVES

Transfer the 4 stitches to the left of the leaf just completed to a needle.

Join a new strand of A and work as for the 1st sepal leaf.

*

PETALS

Transfer the 12 B stitches to 3 needles.

Round 1: Join a 2nd strand of B; with the center facing you and using the double strand of B, knit around—12 double stitches.

Starting at the beginning of the round, transfer every other stitch to 3 holders (4 stitches on each) held to the center for the interior petals; transfer the remaining 12 stitches to 3 holders in a different color (4 stitches on each) held to the outside for the exterior petals, offsetting the exterior petals from the interior petals by 2 stitches. There should be 3 groups of 4 stitches that line up with the sepal leaves and 3 groups of 4 stitches that fall between the sepal leaves.

Cut the yarn and tie the ends in a square knot. Weave in the ends to add structure to the flower foundation, careful so they are woven into like-color fields.

1st Petal

Transfer 1 set of 4 stitches to a needle.

Position the flower so that the center is facing you.

Row 1 (RS): Join a new strand of B; k4.

Row 2: P4.

Row 3: K1, LI-R, k2, LI-L, k1—6 stitches.

Rows 4–14: Work in stockinette stitch.

Row 15: Ssk, knit to the end—5 stitches.

Rows 16–18: Work in stockinette stitch.

Row 19: Knit to the last 2 stitches, k2tog—4 stitches.

Rows 20–22: Work in stockinette stitch.

Row 23: Ssk, knit to the end—3 stitches.

Rows 24–30: Work in stockinette stitch.

Row 31: K1, k2tog—2 stitches.

Row 32: P2.

Row 33: Ssk—1 stitch.

Cut the yarn and pull the tail through the remaining stitch to fasten off. Weave in the ends at the apex and base of the petal along the underside of the edge of the petal.

2nd–8th Petals

Work as for the 1st petal.

————————— N O T E —————————

The flowers pictured on page 135 were not wired.

The Projects

Think of the projects that follow as canvases for your flowers, the starting points for creations of your own imagining.

The centerpiece of the Sunflower Infinity Wrap could easily be the Shirley poppy or the star magnolia. Take the flowers off the scarf and sew them to each other for a stunning neck warmer. Change the scale of the "scarf" and it becomes a wreath of violets, a necklace of lesser celandine, the cherry blossom fairy headdress of a little girl, or a jasmine wedding garland for a bride.

Fingerless Gloves are a practical canvas for small-scale blossoms with their stems twined around narrow cables, or use a grouping of diminutive blooms—you will delight in seeing bright flowers at your fingertips even on cold dark days. The Forget-Me-Not Pillow can be adorned with a profusion of any flower or by a single, bold pom-pom chrysanthemum. The Cherry Blossom Pauper's Purse will be just as beautiful covered with lace-weight crocus flowers and chionodoxa, each stem sprouting from the ring of leaves at the base of the purse. The small Creeping Phlox Clutch is the sweet backdrop for a crowd of meadowfoam or a single multiflora rose. The Gossamer Fuchsia Wrap is a simple yet dramatic piece for any lightweight flower. Imagine ylang-ylang dangling from the corners of a butter-yellow wrap or a smattering of periwinkle decorating the entirety of a white one.

Changing the scale of the flowers through the microscope of gauge also ignites possibilities: Constellations of flowers become voluptuous curtain tie-backs. A single lace-weight flower is sufficient decoration for exquisite place cards at an intimate gathering. Grow knitted sunflowers on the walls of a child's bedroom. Bring spring to the table by decorating sculptural branches with unexpected lilies.

May Violets Fingerless Gloves

DIFFICULTY LEVEL

Gloves: 🌢🌢🌢🌢
Wood Violets: 🌢🌢🌢🌢

SIZES

One size fits most
For a slightly smaller pair of gloves that requires only 1 skein of yarn, make the gloves without the button plackets: Simply seam up the side using a standard mattress stitch.

FINISHED MEASUREMENTS

Circumference (including button plackets, buttoned): 7" (18cm)
Length: 10¼" (26cm)

MATERIALS

Gloves
2 skeins Jade Sapphire *Mongolian Cashmere 4-ply* in Tea Leaves #97
(3) light
Size 4 (3.5mm) needles or size needed to obtain gauge
Twelve ⅜" (10mm) ceramic pearl-style buttons by Creative Impressions in Clay
Twelve ¼–⅜" (6–10mm) mother-of-pearl or other buttons as button stabilizers

Flower Decorations
Stonehedge Fiber Mill *Shepherd's Wool* (fingering weight) 1 skein each of Lime and Spring Green (A) and Lilac and White (B) (1) super fine
Size 0 (2mm) double-pointed needles (set of 5)

(optional) 2mm seed beads in iridescent white, pale green, and aubergine
Cable needle
Sharp large-eyed needle
Sewing and/or beading needle(s)
Sewing and/or fine-gauge nylon beading thread

GAUGE FOR GLOVES

24 stitches and 36 rows = 4" (10cm) in stockinette stitch
To save time, take time to check gauge.

PATTERN NOTE

The gloves are worked flat and then either seamed with mattress stitch, or as with the gloves pictured, you can close with buttons and incorporate button and buttonhole plackets.

INSTRUCTIONS

RIGHT GLOVE

Cast on 52 stitches.
Row 1 (WS): Purl.
Row 2: K3, p1, k8, [p1, k3] 10 times.
Rows 3–9: Work in the established pattern.
Row 10 (cable row): K3, p1, slip 4 stitches onto a cable needle and hold in back, k4, k4 from the cable needle; [p1, k3] 10 times.
Rows 11–29 and other rows not noted: Work in the established pattern.

Rows 30, 50, and 70: Repeat row 10.
Row 75 (thumbhole): K3, p1, k8; [p1, k3] 4 times; bind off 7 stitches for a thumbhole; work as established to end.
Row 76: Work as established to the bound-off stitches; use a cable cast-on to cast on 7 stitches; work as established to end.
Row 90: Repeat row 10.
Row 100: Bind off using an elastic bind-off, such as a sewn bind-off (page 23).

*

LEFT GLOVE

Cast on 52 stitches.
Row 1 (WS): Purl.
Row 2: [K3, p1] 10 times, k8, p1, k3.
Rows 3–9: Work in the established pattern.
Row 10 (cable row): [k3, p1]10 times; slip 4 stitches onto a cable needle and hold in front, k4, k4 from cable needle; p1, k3.
Rows 11–29 and other rows not noted: Work in established pattern.
Rows 30, 50, and 70: Repeat row 10.
Row 75 (thumbhole): [K3, p1] 4; bind off the next 7 stitches for a thumbhole; work in established pattern to end.
Row 76: Work as established to bound-off stitches; use a cable cast-on to cast on 7 stitches; work as established to end.

Row 90: Repeat row 10.

Row 100: Bind off using an elastic bind-off, such as the sewn bind-off.

*

BUTTON PLACKET (OPTIONAL)

With the right side facing, pick up and knit 75 stitches along the noncabled edge.

Row 1 (WS): P3, *k1, p3; repeat from * to the end.

Row 2: K3, *p1, k3; repeat from * to the end.

Repeat rows 1 and 2 until the piece measures ½" (13mm), ending with a wrong-side row.

Next row (RS): Bind off all stitches using an elastic bind-off, such as the sewn bind-off.

*

BUTTONHOLE PLACKET (OPTIONAL)

With the right side facing, pick up and knit 75 stitches along the cabled edge.

Row 1 (WS): P3, *k1, p3; repeat from * to the end.

Row 2 (buttonhole row): K3, p1, k3; *yo, ssk, k2, [p1, k3] twice; repeat from * 4 more times; yo, ssk, k2, p1, k3.

Row 3: Repeat row 1.

Rows 4 and 5: Work the rib as established.

Bind off using the sewn bind-off.

FINISHING

Weave in all ends; then block pieces as necessary.

If opting for no buttons, sew the side seams using mattress stitch.

If opting for buttons, sew the main buttons to the right side of the plackets opposite the buttonholes; sew button stabilizers to the wrong side at the same time.

*

FLORAL DECORATION

Make 6 wood violets—3 White flowers with Lime stems; 3 White flowers with Spring Green stems. Make 2 Lilac flowers, 1 with a Lime stem and one with a Spring Green stem. One glove should have 3 Lime-stemmed violets and 1 Spring Green–stemmed violet, with the remaining 4 violets for the other glove. Tuck the violet stems into the cable crosses and secure the blossoms and stems with sewing thread as necessary. The pictured gloves were hand-beaded with 2mm seed beads in iridescent white (for white flowers), pale green (for stems), and aubergine (for purple violets and the gloves themselves). These were applied using the same method for applying flowers (page 165).

Forget-Me-Not Pillow

DIFFICULTY LEVEL

Pillow: 🌿 🌿 🌿

Forget-Me-Nots: 🌿 🌿 🌿 🌿

FINISHED FELTED MEASUREMENTS

Pillow

24" (61cm) square

MATERIALS

Pillow

8 skeins Stonehedge Fiber Mill *Shepherd's Wool* (worsted weight) in Milk Chocolate **3** light

Size 11 (8mm) 24" (61cm) circular needles (2) or size needed to obtain gauge

Stitch marker

26" (66cm) square pillow form

18" (45.5cm) or longer brown zipper

Tapestry needle

Sewing needle

Sewing or nylon beading thread

Flower Decorations

1 skein each of Stonehedge Fiber Mill *Shepherd's Wool* (worsted weight) in White (A & B), Misty Blue (C), Light Turquoise (C), and Baby Blue (C) **3** light

Size 6 (4mm) double-pointed needles (set)

Locking stitch markers (as stitch holders)

Darning needle

Sewing thread

GAUGE FOR PILLOW

Prefelted gauge: 12 stitches and 16 rounds = 4" (10cm) in stockinette stitch using a double strand of yarn (before felting)

Felted gauge: 16 stitches and 28 rounds = 4" (10cm) in stockinette stitch using a double strand of yarn (after felting)

PATTERN NOTES

- Two circular needles are required to begin and end the square pillow.
- The pillow is knit with 2 strands of yarn held together.
- To make an unfelted pillow, choose a yarn (or 2 strands of a smaller-gauge yarn held together) with needles that will achieve the "felted" stitch gauge given above. Use the instructions as written here.

INSTRUCTIONS

PILLOW

Bottom Edge

Cast on 96 stitches; do not join.

Row 1: Purl.

Row 2 (increase row): Kfb in each stitch across—192 stitches.

Divide the stitches: Slip the 1st and every other (odd) stitch onto the right point of the circular needle (held toward the front) and the 2nd and every other (even) stitch onto a 2nd circular needle (held toward the back)—96 stitches each needle. These 2 sets of stitches will form the pillow front and back.

Body

Hold the 2 needles so that the ridge formed by the first 2 rows of knitting is on the top edge of the fabric—as you work, the two needles will enclose

this ridge so that it is on the inside of the pillow—and begin knitting in the round with the 2 circular needles, marking the beginning of the round. Knit 168 rounds, changing to a single circular needle when it is comfortable to do so.

Top Edge and Opening

Slip the first 96 stitches onto a 2nd circular needle.

Turn the pillow inside out so that the 2 right sides are together.

Last row (WS): Using a 3-needle bind-off, bind off the first 14 stitches; create an opening by binding off the center stitches of each side separately as follows: With the wrong side facing, bind off the next 68 stitches knitwise; bind off the last 14 stitches using a 3-needle bind-off. Weave in all ends.

Finishing

Felt the pillow using the directions for larger felted articles found in Felting Basics (page 160) until the pillow reaches the finished measurements listed at the beginning of the pattern. Once the felted pillow is pulled into shape, sew the zipper into the opening following the instructions for inserting zippers in pillows on page 166. For the best results, sew the zipper in place while the bag is damp.

＊

FLORAL DECORATIONS

Make 23 forget-me-nots (see page 68) as follows: 10 flowers in White (A and B) and Misty Blue (C);

6 flowers in White (A and B) and Light Turquoise (C), and 7 flowers in White (A and B) and Baby Blue (C).

Finishing

Before the pillow is stuffed, lay it out on a large flat surface. Arrange your flowers on the pillow so that they are nicely spaced and the colors appear to be evenly distributed over the front. Once the flowers are arranged as you desire, pin each flower in place using long (strong) straight pins—take care to pin through only 1 thickness of the pillow and through the center of the flower for best results.

Measure a double length of sewing thread about 30" (76cm) long. Thread the double strand of sewing thread on a darning needle, and sew each flower in place. Begin by securing the center of each flower. To do this, make invisible stitches around the perimeter of the flower center using the basic method for applying flowers (page 165). Then secure the flower petals to the pillow with a single stitch to the center of each. There is no need to secure the perimeter of each petal unless your forget-me-not pillow is for an exuberant child.

It is a good idea to sew the flowers to the pillow while the flowers are still damp—this way the stitches function to block the flowers in just the way you have sewn them down.

Sunflower Infinity Wrap

DIFFICULTY LEVEL
Wrap: ◊ ◊ ◊ ◊
Sunflowers: ◊ ◊ ◊ ◊

FINISHED MEASUREMENTS
6" (15cm) wide x 120" (305cm) long

MATERIALS
Wrap
Red Barn Yarn *Worsted Weight* : 3 skeins
in Nora No. 7 (dark chocolate brown)
【4】 medium
Size 7 (4.5mm) 24 or 32" (60 or
80cm) circular needle or size needed
to obtain gauge

Flower Decorations
Each flower requires approximately 35
yards (32m) of A, 20 yards (18m) of
B, 40 yards (37m) of C, and 20 yards
(18m) of D.
Size 7 (4.5mm) 16" (40cm) circular
needle
Size 7 (4.5mm) double-pointed
needles (set of 5)

**FOR THE PICTURED WRAP,
MAKE 3 SUNFLOWERS US-
ING THE FOLLOWING YARN
BRANDS AND COLORS:**

Plymouth Yarns *Galway Worsted* Apple
Green #127 (A), Bark Heather #757
(B), and Lemon Zest #179 (C)
【3】 light
Crystal Palace *Fizz* Mink #7342 (D)
【1】 super fine
Stonehedge Fiber Mill *Shepherd's Wool*

(worsted weight) Sage (A), Brown (B),
and Roasted Pumpkin (C) 【3】 light
Crystal Palace *Fizz* Mink #7342 (D)
【1】 super fine
Stonehedge Fiber Mill *Shepherd's Wool*
(worsted weight) Sage (A), Brown (B),
and Harvest Gold (C) 【3】 light
Crystal Palace *Fizz* Mink #7342 (D)
【1】 super fine

GAUGE FOR INFINITY WRAP
20 stitches and 24 rounds = 4" (10cm)
in stockinette stitch
To save time, take time to check gauge.

INSTRUCTIONS

With D, cast on 162 stitches.
Place a marker for the beginning of
the round and join, taking care not to
twist the stitches.
Rounds 1–12: Work in stockinette
stitch.
Rounds 13–24: Work in reverse
stockinette stitch.
Repeat rounds 1–24 four more
times—piece should measure 20"
(51cm)].
Work 12 rounds in stockinette stitch—
piece should measure 22" (56cm).
Bind off all stitches using a sewn bind-
off (page 23).

FLOWER DECORATIONS
Make 3 flowers following instructions
on page 124.

*

FINISHING
Place flowers in lingerie bags and
felt as desired (refer to page 160
for information about felting flowers).
Using a double strand of sewing
thread that matches the wrap and
a sharp sewing needle, hand-sew
flowers to the infinity wrap using
invisible stitches.

Gossamer Fuchsia Wrap

DIFFICULTY LEVEL

Wrap: 🌢 🌢 🌢 🌢

Fuchsia: 🌢 🌢 🌢 🌢

FINISHED MEASUREMENTS

Wrap

Length: 75" (190cm)

Width: 10" (25.5cm)

Note: I did not block this wrap, in order to allow the natural ruched effect of the smaller-gauge stitches to emerge.

MATERIALS

Wrap

2 skeins Shibui *Silk Cloud* in Peony #220 (B) (🔟) lace

Size 1 (2.25mm) needles or needle size to obtain gauge

Size 13 (9mm) needles or needle size to obtain gauge

Flower Decorations

1 skein each Shibui *Silk Cloud* in Wasabi #7495 (A), Peony #220 (B), and Blossom #1765 (C) (🔟) lace

Size 1 (2.25mm) needles

Fine-gauge sharp needle

Sewing and/or beading needle(s)

Sewing and/or fine-gauge nylon beading thread

GAUGE FOR WRAP

28 stitches and 80 rows = 4" (10cm) in garter stitch using smaller needles

12 stitches and 10 rows = 4" (10cm) in garter stitch using larger needles

To save time, take time to check gauge.

WRAP

With B and smaller needles, cast on 70 stitches.

Rows 1–10: Work in garter stitch.

Rows 11–15: Change to larger needles and work in garter stitch for 5 rows.

Work [rows 1–15] 30 times total or number of times to reach desired length—450 rows.

Change to smaller needles and work 10 rows.

Bind off all stitches using the sewn bind-off (page 23).

Finishing

Block to finished measurements.

✳

FLOWER DECORATIONS

Make 4 single fuchsias and 2 double fuchsias to decorate the ends of the wrap (refer to page 69 for the fuchsia flower instructions).

Finishing

Sew flowers to ends of wrap.

Cherry Blossom Pauper's Purse

DIFFICULTY LEVEL

Purse: 🌿🌿🌿🌿
Flowers & Leaves: 🌿🌿🌿🌿

PURSE FINISHED MEASUREMENTS

9½" (24cm) wide at opening x 11½" (29cm) tall from top to tip (excluding tassel)

MATERIALS

Purse
2 skeins Tilli Tomas *Plié* in Parchment (A) (3) light
Size 4 (3.5mm) 16" (40.5cm) circular needle or size needed to obtain gauge
Stitch marker
Fine-gauge sewing or beading needle
Sewing or beading thread

Flower Decorations
1 skein each Tilli Tomas *Beaded Plié* in Romance (B), American Beauty (C), and Washington (D) (3) light
Size 4 (3.5mm) double-pointed needles (set of 5)

GAUGE FOR PURSE

26 stitches and 32 rounds = 4" (10cm) in stockinette stitch
To save time, take time to check gauge.

SPECIAL TECHNIQUE

Picot Cast-on: Using a knitted cast-on method, *cast 5 stitches onto the left-hand needle; bind off 2 cast-on stitches—1 stitch remains on the right-hand needle; slip the remaining stitch back onto the left needle; repeat from * until all stitches have been cast on.

PATTERN NOTE

Change to double-pointed needles when the stitches no longer fit comfortably on the circular needle.

INSTRUCTIONS

PURSE

With the circular needle and A, cast on 120 stitches using picot cast-on; mark the beginning of the round and join, taking care not to twist the stitches.

Work in k4, p1 rib until the piece measures approximately 2" (5cm).

Eyelet round: *K2tog, yo; repeat from * around—120 stitches.

Knit all rounds until the piece measures approximately 10" (25.5cm).

Next round: *K20, place marker; repeat from * around.

Round 1 (decrease round): *K1, k2tog, knit to 3 stitches before next marker, ssk, k1, slip marker; repeat from * around—108 stitches.

Round 2: Knit around.

Rounds 3–16: Repeat [rounds 1 and 2] 7 more times—24 stitches.

Round 17 (decrease round): *Ssk, k2tog, slip marker; repeat from * around—12 stitches.

Round 18 (decrease round): Removing marker, k2tog around—6 stitches.

Cut yarn, leaving a tail of approximately 15" (38cm). Thread tail through the remaining stitches and pull tight. Do not cut.

Finishing
Tassels (make 1 for bag bottom and 2 for drawstring handles)

Cut a 6" (15cm) square out of cardboard as a template for creating the tassels.

Tassel Body: Wrap C snugly (but not so tightly as to bend the template) around the cardboard 30 times. Wrap more times for a beefier tassel.

Tassel Loop: Cut another strand of C 10" (25.5cm) long. Pass this strand between the tassel yarn and the cardboard and slide it to the top edge of the cardboard, then pull it tight around the tassel. Using a square knot (right over left, left over right), tie the strand securely around the top of the tassel. Insert sharp scissors between the tassel and the cardboard at the bottom edge—right on the

edge—and cut the yarn carefully.
Tassel "Waist": Cut a 10" (25.5cm) strand of C and wrap it around the tassel about ½" (13mm) from the top. Tie the 2 ends of this wrapped yarn together in a square knot and weave the tails to the inside of the tassel so that they aren't visible. At this point, if the bottom edge of the tassel isn't quite even, even out the ends by holding the tassel by the loop and cutting slowly and evenly along the bottom edge.
Drawstring Handle: Cut two 1-yd (1m) double strands of C. Use a tapestry needle to thread 1 double strand through the eyelet holes at the top of the bag, ending where you began. Thread the other double strand through the eyelet holes so that it begins and ends exactly opposite the 1st double-strand handle.

Attach a tassel to the open drawstring end by using the drawstring yarn to create the tassel "loop."

Secure with a square knot, and then thread the raw ends into the tassel itself to hide them. Cut the ends to the tassel length as necessary.

FLOWER DECORATIONS
Make 4 cherry blossoms in B and 3 blossoms in C (see page 43).

Cherry Leaves (make 15)
With D, cast on 1 stitch.
Row 1 (RS): Kfbf—3 stitches.
Row 2: P, k1, p1.
Row 3: Kfb, p1, kfb—5 stitches.
Row 4: P2, k1, p2.
Row 5: Kfb, kfb, p1, kfb, kfb—9 stitches.
Row 6: P4, k1, p4.
Row 7: Kfb, k3, p1, k3, kfb—11 stitches.
Rows 8–12: Work the stitches you see (WS: P5, k1, p5; RS: k5, p1, k5).
Row 13: Ssk, k3, p1, k3, k2tog—9 stitches.
Row 14: P4, k1, p4.
Row 15: Ssk, k2, p1, k2, k2tog—7 stitches.
Row 16: P2tog, p1, k1, p1, ssp—5 stitches.
Row 17: Ssk, p1, k2tog—3 stitches.
Row 18: Sl 1, p2tog, psso—1 stitch.
Cut the yarn. Pull the end through the remaining stitch to fasten off. Weave in the ends.

*

FINISHING
Arrange the flowers on the bag and pin in place. With a double strand of polyester sewing thread or thin-gauge nylon beading thread and a sharp sewing needle, sew in place with small, precise stitches.

DIFFICULTY LEVEL

Bag: 🖊 🖊 🖊 🖊
Flowers: 🖊 🖊 🖊 🖊

FINISHED MEASUREMENTS FOR BAG

Height: 7½" (19cm)
Width (front and back faces) at top: 6" (15cm)
Width (front and back faces) at bottom: 6¾" (17cm)
Depth: 2" (5cm)

MATERIALS

Bag
Stonehedge Fiber Mill *Shepherd's Wool* (worsted weight): 1 skein of Black (A) **⊕3** light
Size 8 (5mm) 16" (40.5cm) circular needles or size needed to obtain gauge
4 stitch markers, 1 a different color for the beginning of the round
7" (18cm) Lucite purse frame
20 tiny black seed beads

Flower Decorations
1 skein ArtYarns *Beaded Rhapsody* in #148 S (B); this is a variegated white-to-gray-to-black yarn with silver metallic thread and tiny clear seed beads **⊕4** medium
Size 4 (3.5mm) double-pointed needles (set of 5)
Four 7mm and seven 10mm clear sparkle rivets

GAUGE FOR BAG

16 stitches and 22 rounds = 4" (10cm) in stockinette stitch (before felting)
16 stitches and 24 rounds = 4" (10cm) in stockinette stitch (after felting)

NOTE

Please check your pre-felted and felted gauges by swatching and shrinking an 8" x 8" (20.5cm x 20.5cm) square first. There will be some variation in finished size if gauge differs due to different needle size, yarn type, or fiber content.

PATTERN NOTES

• Make 11 blossoms for 1 side of the bag. Some people may like only the front of the bag to be decorated while others will prefer to make 22 blossoms and decorate both sides of the bag (see page 52 for creeping phlox flower instructions).

• When using variegated yarn, as I did, you must pay attention to the moment in the color repeat that you begin each flower. For greatest flower uniformity, begin each flower at the same point and then begin each flower petal at the same point. Because the color repeat for Beaded Rhapsody is fairly short, it worked beautifully for the creeping phlox flower, though I did have to sacrifice some short bits in order to begin the petals at the right location in the color repeat.

INSTRUCTIONS

BAG BOTTOM

With A, cast on 40 stitches.
Work in stockinette stitch for 16 rows.
Bind off all stitches using the sewn bind-off (page 23).

*

BAG BODY

With the right side facing, pick up and knit stitches as follows: *40 stitches along the long side, 12 stitches along the short end; repeat from * once more, join and k1; place a marker for the beginning of the round—104 stitches.

Round 1: *K38, place a marker, k14, place a marker; repeat from * once more (the beginning-of-round marker is the last marker).

Rounds 2–9: Knit.

Shape the short end as follows:

Round 10 (decrease round): *Knit to the next marker, slip the marker, ssk, knit to 2 stitches before the next marker, k2tog; repeat from * once—100 stitches.

Rounds 11–15: Continue to knit in the round.

Rounds 16, 22, 28, 34: Repeat round 10, knit all other rounds not noted—84 stitches after last decrease.

Rounds 35–39: Knit, ending the last round 2 stitches before the beginning-of-round marker.

Round 40: Removing the markers, *k2tog, knit to the next marker, ssk; repeat from * once—80 stitches.

BAG FLAPS

Row 1 (RS): K40; join a new strand of yarn and k40.

Continue working each flap simultaneously as follows:

Rows 2–4: Work in stockinette stitch.

Row 5: *K1, ssk, knit to the last 3 stitches, k2tog, k1—38 stitches each flap.

Rows 6–8: Work in stockinette stitch.

Row 9: Repeat row 5—36 stitches each flap.

Rows 10–12: Work in stockinette stitch.

Row 13: Repeat row 5—34 stitches each flap.

Rows 14–16: Work in stockinette stitch.

Row 17: Repeat row 5—32 stitches each flap.

Row 18: Purl.

Bind off all stitches.

*

FELTING

Refer to page 160 for specific instructions for felting the bag.

The pictured purse frame has a slot into which the felted flap must be placed. I used a long, large-gauge darning needle for this purpose. Push the flap into the slot with the sharp end of the needle. Once the flap is placed properly, use a fine-gauge sharp sewing needle and a double strand of nylon beading thread to sew the felted purse flaps to the purse frame as follows: Begin on the inside of the purse frame at 1 end. Insert the threaded needle through the 1st hole and sew through all thicknesses. Thread a seed bead onto the thread and then insert the needle back into the same hole to secure. Sew through all thicknesses again. Travel to the next hole on the inside of the purse frame. Continue in this manner until the frame and flap are secured together. Repeat for remaining side. Snap closed.

*

SPECIAL CREEPING PHLOX INSTRUCTIONS

These phlox flowers have concave centers and short stems specially designed to hold the sparkle rivet centers.

Receptacle (flower foundation)

With B, cast on 5 stitches.

Round 1: Knit across; without turning your work, slip the row to the other end of the needle; pull the yarn across the back to begin round 2 below.

Round 2: Knit around. Divide the stitches between 2 needles.

Round 3: Purl around; W&T.

Round 4: Position the flower so that the center of the flower is now facing you. The 1st stitch worked in this round was the last stitch worked in the previous round. You are now working in the opposite direction from the previous round. Kfb in each stitch—10 stitches. The right side has now switched so that the flower petals will now face right side up.

Round 5: Knit around. Cut the yarn and weave in the ends.

Transfer the 8 stitches to 4 holders (2 stitches on each); keep 2 stitches on a needle to work the 1st petal.

1st Petal

Position the flower so that the petal undersides are facing away from you and the flower center is facing you.

Row 1 (RS): Join a new strand of B; k1, M1, k1—3 stitches.

Row 2: P3.

Row 3: K1, kfb, k1—4 stitches.

Row 4: P4.

Row 5: K2, M1, k2—5 stitches.

Rows 6–8: Work in stockinette stitch.

Row 9: K2, bind off 1, k2.

Row 10: *P2, turn, k2tog, cut the yarn and draw the end through the remaining stitch; join a new strand and repeat from * once on the remaining 2 stitches.

Weave in the ends along the underside edge base and tips of the petals so that the petal tips appear blunt and rounded.

2nd–5th Petals

Transfer the 2 stitches to the left of the petal just completed to a needle. Join a new strand of B and work as for the 1st petal.

FINISHING

The pictured flowers were decorated with clear sparkle rivets. Place the fancy (male) part of the rivet in the center of each flower; next, place the female part of the rivet onto the male part on the flower back and press together until you hear a click. Place the rivet face on a padded surface (I used several cardboard coasters or a magazine for this purpose), and use a hammer to secure the rivet together. Position flowers so that they create a mass of creeping phlox on one or both sides of the bag. Pin each flower in place. Sew onto the bag using a double strand of nylon beading thread and a sharp sewing needle, tacking centers and petal edges as necessary for the desired look.

Appendix

Felting Basics

While each of the flowers in this book looks beautiful simply knitted, felting them not only adds structure but it enhances the suspension of disbelief. The star magnolia, for example, is beautiful with wired petals. Once felted, however, it becomes ethereal.

THE PHYSICS OF FELTING

The shaft of the woolen fiber has small scales on it that, when agitated, lock with other scales on other woolen fibers and matt or "felt" together. These scales can be stripped way by chemical processes to create superwash wool that will not felt no matter how many times you wash it.

While we often think of washing woolens in order to felt them (or woolens felting when we least want them to!), washing them in a washing machine is not the only way to get wool to felt. Agitation of any sort is all that's necessary to make natural wool fibers matt together. Wool can be sanded, rolled between the palms of your hands, dragged behind a wagon, or beaten to a felt. Hot water, a little soap, and the agitator in a washing machine make it easy, but only for projects that fall within a certain size range. For larger projects, such as buildings and rugs, wool fibers are piled up to the requisite thickness and beaten with sticks made for this specific purpose. Some contemporary artists spread out great sheets of wool fibers, wet them, lay down a protective cloth, and then get out the floor sander to sand the fibers into matting.

While the flowers represented here can be made out of yarn with any fiber content, from silk to mink to milk to mohair, according to the desires of the knitter, if they are made out of wool, they can also be felted, and doing so can give the flowers greater verisimilitude. Thus, we will be felting knitted objects. The technical term for felting knitted fabric is "fulling," but most contemporary knitters refer to it as "felting," so this is the term I will also use.

THE METHODS OF FELTING

Before you begin, test your yarn for colorfastness to limit possible color bleeding. To do this, make a small swatch (a 2" x 2" [5cm x 5cm] knitted swatch will do the trick) and drop it in boiling-hot water. Yarn that is not colorfast will almost immediately begin to shed color like a teabag dropped into hot water. See below for how to treat your knitted items *before felting*, so as to preserve color.

Felting in Conventional (Non–High Efficiency [HE]) Top-Loading Washers

To felt knitted items, put larger pieces in separate lingerie bag(s) or zippered pillow protector(s). For small flowers, multiples may be put in the same bag unless they have long stems that might tie themselves in knots or tie themselves around other flowers and stems. In this case, put flowers in a zippered bag that is just slightly bigger than the flower you are felting. Make larger bags smaller by tying knots in them.

Put your piece(s) in the smallest load size that accommodates the project and allows it to move freely. Most flowers, even multiples, should be put in an extra-small or small load size. The small felted clutch (see page 154) can also be put in a small load size.

Add tennis balls, sport shoes devoted to felting, or a soft canvas bag that is devoted to felting. Do not use towels or other items that will release lint onto your felt. Choose the hot/cold water setting and add a tiny bit of soap—soap creates an alkaline environment and this causes the wool fibers to swell and their scales to lift up and so more readily interlock with other fibers when agitated. Check often to see how things are coming along. If you're felting flowers, open the bags and check the shape of the petals and the stitch definition to make sure stems are not getting tangled. If you're felting knitted bags, make sure they are not getting creased and that they are moving around freely. Pull bags into shape so that they felt evenly and check measurements and felt density so that you do not overfelt.

To conserve resources, turn back the agitation dial until felting is complete, rather than letting the machine complete multiple cycles. When the flowers and/or bags have reached the size you desire, rinse (with no agitation or rinse in cold tap water) and spin dry. Remove and block.

Felting in HE/Front-Loading Washers

I haven't had much experience with the new, high-efficiency washing machines. In the workshops I teach, I've seen many bags and flowers come out of all different sorts of washers, and there are some HE washers that produce lovely felted products—including flowers, bags, and other items. But some are too thorough in their efficiency to produce a good felt. They're simply too good at spinning and so can reduce a flower or bag to a crumple from which it can't recover. Before you put a precious flower or evening bag body in your front-loading washer for the first time, please test an 8" x 8" (20.5cm x 20.5cm) swatch first. If the swatch ends up a crumple, please consider not felting in your washer. In this case, try felting in your clothes dryer (next topic).

If your swatch survived and looks terrific, follow the basic instructions for felting in a top-loading washer (previous topic).

Felting in a Clothes Dryer

Soak your project in boiling-hot water with a drop or two of soap for about 10 minutes. Squeeze out the excess water and then put your piece in the clothes dryer. Felt just as you would in the washer (refer to the top-loader instructions above for the basics): The agitation of the dryer is what causes the felting. Stay close by and check often. Once your flowers or bags have felted to the desired density, stitch definition, or measurements, pull them into shape and wire (page 32) or otherwise block.

Felting by Hand in a Bucket, Sink, or Bathtub

A wonderful knitter named Witt Pratt introduced me to the method of felting in a bucket with a plunger. He remarked that he used this method whenever he had just finished knitting something he intended to felt and was somewhere with no washer. Here, as with other by-hand methods, you'll want to assemble containers of icy water and boiling-hot

water. Also, find or buy a nice new plunger and a clean bucket—or content yourself with the sink or bathtub. It's best to wear thick rubber gloves to protect your hands. Begin by soaking the piece in hot soapy water and working it between your fingers until you feel it begin to thicken. Then begin to agitate it in the bucket with the plunger—the plunger is for agitation, not so much to work on the felt directly. Between bouts of agitation, shock the piece back and forth between hot and cold water. Check frequently to see how the felting process is coming along. Stop when the piece is the feel and thickness you want and there's a desired loss of stitch definition.

Felting by Hand with a Glass Washboard

Begin by assembling the same materials you would for felting by hand in a bucket, sink, or bathtub: a bowl of steaming-hot, just slightly soapy water (only a drop or two of detergent is necessary) and a bowl of icy-cold water. These

bowls, when filled with water, must be deep enough for you to submerge the piece you are felting. Begin by soaking your project in the hot soapy water. Squeeze out some of the excess water and rub vigorously against the glass washboard, emphasizing different parts of the piece as you do so. When you get a little frustrated, dunk your piece into the cold water, then back into the hot, then rub some more. After a little bit, perhaps just as you begin to wonder if it will ever felt, you'll begin to feel the piece stiffen—the felting process will be faster now that things are getting going. Continue to alternate shocking the piece in cold water, then hot water, then squeezing out a little of the excess water and rubbing vigorously on the washboard.

TROUBLESHOOTING COMMON PROBLEMS

Of course, it's best to read this section before you have to do any troubleshooting, so as to avoid the whole issue, but sometimes things happen. Those tomatoes really needed staking right as you started felting, the phone rang, your toddler ran out the front door with just froggie boots on . . . or a well-meaning friend offered to felt something for you and it didn't turn out quite as you expected.

1. Color Migration or Bleeding

If you felt multiple flowers or bags that are different colors together, fibers from each of the projects will visit and become attached elsewhere. So, your lovely white Oriental lily might end up covered with black fibers from that cute little evening bag. If this happens, you can pick some of the fibers out by hand and others with tweezers.

Best, however, to avoid the whole thing! Felt like colors together to avoid fiber migration and its cousin, bleeding. Only worse than the Oriental lily with dark fibers spoiling its whiteness is the one that comes out of the wash positively gray from that same little bag (now itself spoiled by little white fibers).

Here are several things you can do if you are working with a yarn brand or dye lot that is not as colorfast as you would like: Soak the item to be felted in a vinegar bath (¼ cup [50ml] distilled white vinegar to a gallon [4l] of cool water), rinse, then felt using the desired method.

Felt the item by itself in the smallest load size that will accommodate the project and still allow it to move around freely.

Felt with a "color catcher." I haven't used these much, since I tend to avoid felting different colors together, but some folks report great success with them. They can be found at the local supermarket in the laundry detergent aisle.

2. Uneven Felting

This is more likely to be a problem with a giant flower, bag, or some other larger item than it is with small, single-strand, worsted- or lace-weight flowers. If you've felted a bag or supersized daffodil and found that it looks a bit creased here and there, rather than as smooth as you expected, you can often rewet and refelt if it's not already too densely felted.

Check the load size: Most unevenness is the result of a load size that is too small for the size of the project or the result of what I will delicately refer to as "the felter's error" (see the Watch it! And Bag it! tips that follow).

Watch it!: You must watch what you felt. I recommend that you stay by the washer or dryer and check that the felting process is going along smoothly. If you are the sort of person who must go out and stake up that fallen tomato while something is felting (as I have done, to my own chagrin), beware lest you regret it! The tomatoes will wait until your flowers are felted to your liking. At this point I must reiterate the importance of removing your flowers or bags from the washer or dryer frequently to inspect them: The bigger the project, the more important this is. Whereas with flowers you can probably just check them every so often and take them out of agitation as soon as they lose stitch definition, bags and giant flowers require a lot more attention.

Bag it!: Use lingerie or other zippered bags to protect delicate flowers and I-cords from the violence of the washer. Bags also limit how furry certain yarns become. It is simply a fact of using dyed yarns that the darker dyes sometimes cause the yarn to shed a lot during the agitation process. Felting purses and flowers in bags not only helps you keep them from getting too furry but it helps prevent all that furriness from getting into your washer.

3. Density Problems: It's Too Floppy or Too Thick and Stiff...

Too floppy? If your flowers or bags come out of the washer too floppy, this can be remedied with another round of agitation—not always a complete cycle, mind you, unless it's necessary. It's better not to think in terms of the washer's cycles but to let the felting tell you when it's done. So you should felt as long as it's necessary to do so for you to be supremely happy with your work, but not a moment longer. It may be that you decide something is too floppy after it has dried and even been used in its floppy state. Not to worry. You can rewet and refelt again as many times as it takes for you to achieve the desired results. Some yarns simply take longer than others to felt to your liking.

Too thick and stiffly felted? This is harder to deal with than too floppy and best to be avoided in the first place. But maybe you didn't take me seriously when I said to forget about the tomatoes that need staking up until after the felting is done. Worsted-weight flowers, small as they are, take longer to felt than bags or supersized flowers and are, therefore, most *unlikely* to be overfelted. More *likely*, you'll get tired of turning back the agitation dial and take them out before all stitch definition is gone. Bags and big flowers, however, because of their increased surface area (greater surface area = faster, thicker felting) are more easily overfelted. Some yarns, particularly those with a high-merino content, are quick felters and so prone to overfelting without a watchful felter standing by.

Overfelted? If you have overfelted a bag that was meant to be sewn to a frame of a certain size, find a new frame that is smaller. Or view it as an opportunity to activate your creativity. Some will throw the poor thing away in disgust and knit it again. That approach has its merits, too. If the bag is close to fitting the frame, I say wet it and stretch it with something appropriate, such as a board just the right size, a sturdy box. . . . Look around—you'll find something. Let it dry in this stretched state. Or let it mostly dry and then finish it while it's still just slightly damp.

With flowers, a good job of wiring and blocking can often disguise a thick felt.

4. High Plumbing Bills Due to Excess Wool Lint in the Washer

It's a danger when felting in the clothes washer that too much of the wool lint will either gum up the washer works or gum up your pipes. I've suffered from the latter in the past and have since taken precautions to avoid the nastiness of flooding, ruined floors, and visits from the plumber who had to get out the extra-heavy-duty snakes that can only be carried into the house by two men working together. Many washers can be outfitted with a lint trap on the drainage hose that empties into a utility sink, but for folks like me who don't have such a setup due to a washer in a small space, I recommend a felting sieve. I keep it within easy reach and use it whenever I felt. I remove all felted items from the washer and place them in large bowls or plastic bins to drain. I let the water settle for a bit, and as it settles, the wool fibers float to the top of the water. Then I scoop out the fibers for a bit, let the water settle a bit and scoop again. I then drain the water out. Only then do I put my felted flowers or bags back into the washer and set to Spin.

I have had students who did other things to get rid of the lint: Some only used zippered pillow protectors because they do catch more lint. Others put a 1–2 count (that is, you count to 2) of bleach into the water (after all felted items are removed) and let the water sit until the bleach consumes every last wayward fiber. Warning: Do not, at that point, put your felting back into the washer unless you rinse a bit to make sure that all the bleach has been removed.

Honoring Your Work: The Importance of Fine Finishing

APPLYING FLOWERS TO MYRIAD SURFACES

By sewing: It's important to sew flowers to the designated site in a way that shows them off to best effect. When I teach workshops, I implore my students to sew the flower down in the way they want it to be: If you like the petal curving a certain way, sew it that way. If you want the stem to twine a bit, rise up off the pillow, or bag, or coat lapel, sew it that way. You are in control. Make your artistic vision felt.

The basic method of ensuring that flowers don't fall off as you walk down the avenue is to make a few stitches and then make a knot. Just as good pearls, or finer beads masquerading as good pearls, are secured by a knot on either side of the bead, you should secure your flowers with a knot after every few stitches.

To make sure flowers stay put, use a double strand of nylon beading thread and a long, sharp sewing needle. It's fine to sew through all thicknesses and do your traveling where it won't show (such as the inside of a bag that will be lined). If you're sewing to a lapel, for example, where you don't want to have a mass of terrible-looking tacking stitches on the back (just in case you need to put up your collar against a brisk wind), insert your needle at an angle going both from flower and lapel-front surface to back and from back to front. This way you can travel around to tack the flower without any messiness.

Another way of hiding traveling stitches is to insert the needle either into the flower itself (such as when you are sewing a delicate flower to an even more delicate surface, as on the Gossamer Fuchsia Wrap on page 148) or through the surface to which you're sewing the flower. In this example, you need to travel through the architecture of the flower itself to the next point where you would like to tack the flower to the wrap. Because both flowers and wrap are so delicate, it's best to use either an invisible sewing thread, such as a filament thread, or sewing thread that's the same color as the portion of the flower body you're traveling through.

Another example: If you're sewing a flower to a bag that *will not* be lined, you may want to travel from the site of one tacking stitch to another *through* the felt itself, in a mole-like fashion. Wherever you want to make a tacking stitch, come out on the inside of the bag, go through all thicknesses, insert needle almost where you came out on the bag or flower and go through all thicknesses to the inside again. Make a securing knot, and then insert the needle back into the felt and travel to the site of the next tacking stitch, coming out on the inside again.

By pinning: You may want to move flowers around or give them as gifts. In this case, it may be most appropriate to pin them. Actually affix a pin-back to the back of your flower so that it may be worn as a pin. For large flowers, you'll need more than one pin-back in order to distribute the weight of the flower evenly over a larger surface area. You may also need to tack the petals together as you would have them lie so that you remain in control of the flower long after it has been received by your grateful friend.

By gluing: People often ask me if I ever glue flowers to bags or other fabric surfaces. Frankly, no. If I want to move the flower around, I pin. I'll even staple in a pinch, but for anything meant to last, I will always opt for sewing flowers to a bag or garment. However, if I want to affix flowers to the top of a beautiful gift box made of cardboard or wood, gluing might be the best solution. In this case, find a good fabric glue and follow the manufacturer's instructions.

Inserting a Zipper in the Forget-Me-Not Pillow

The first step in sewing in the zipper is picking the correct zipper. Select a zipper that has large teeth and matches the pillow color. I like large-tooth plastic zippers that come in a range of colors.

1. FIT THE ZIPPER TO THE PILLOW OPENING

Make the zipper just a little longer than the pillow opening. Start either with a zipper that has been made to fit the opening (finish off the bottom end with metal clips specifically for this purpose)—available at full-service fabric shops and specialty stores—or use sewing thread to hand-sew (or machine-zigzag in place) over and around the zipper teeth to shorten the zipper.

Cut off the excess, leaving an end that measures ½–1" (13mm–2.5cm) long.

2. PREPARE AND ALIGN THE PILLOW OPENING

It's critical that you align the 2 sides of the opening before sewing the zipper in place, lest you get a twist in the body of the pillow. Place the pillow on a flat surface so that the 2 sides of the opening come together in the center and are perfectly aligned from end to end. Every 2–3" (5–7.5cm), starting 1" (2.5cm) from each end, place pairs of sewing pins on both sides of the pillow opening so that they "match up" along the entire length.

What you are doing is creating a reference point for the alignment of the zipper.

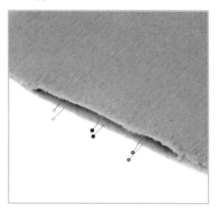

3. PIN ONE SIDE OF THE ZIPPER AND SEW IN PLACE

Without unzipping the zipper, pin 1 side in place, placing these pins parallel to the pillow opening on the inside of the pillow so that they do not interfere with the ones you are using to align the pillow opening.

Sew the 1st side of the zipper in place using a double strand of like-colored nylon beading thread. Use running stitches on the inside of the pillow/underside of the zipper and tiny stitches on the pillow exterior that will be invisible when pulled tight.

4. MATCH THE SECOND SIDE OF THE ZIPPER AND SEW IN PLACE

Once you have finished sewing the 1st side in place, place pins in the 2nd side of the zipper that align with their corresponding pin markers in the pillow opening.

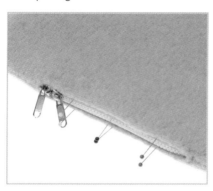

Unzip the zipper, pin the 2nd side of the zipper in place. Before *sewing* in place, however, zip the zipper to ensure that it is correctly aligned.

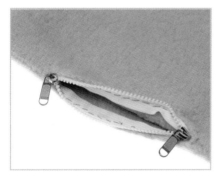

If not, adjust, repin, and recheck before again unzipping the zipper and completing the final step.

Sew the 2nd side of the zipper in place as you did the 1st. Remove the pins as you go. At this point, I zip and unzip that zipper several times, as it gives me a terrific sense of satisfaction.

Yarn Information

What follows is a comprehensive index of the yarns used in this book. Nevertheless, the flowers here can be made in virtually any yarn. The yarns listed below are but a starting point or a sampling of possibilities.

Alpaca with a Twist *Baby Twist* (double-knitting weight; 100% alpaca; 110 yds [100m] per 1¾ oz [50g] ball) **3** light

Alpaca with a Twist *Fino* (fingering weight; 70% alpaca, 30% silk; 875 yds [800m] per 3½ oz [100g] skein) **1** super fine

ArtYarns *Beaded Rhapsody* (worsted weight; 85% silk with glass beads and metallic thread, 15% mohair; 175 yds [160m] per 3½ oz [100g] skein) **4** medium

Crystal Palace *Fizz* (100% polyester; 120 yds [110m] per 1¾ oz [50g] ball) **1** super fine

Jade Sapphire *Mongolian Cashmere* 4-ply (double-knitting weight; 100% cashmere; 200 yds [183m] per 1½ oz [55g] skein) **3** light

Nashua Handknits *Creative Focus Bulky* (heavy worsted; 75% wool, 25% alpaca; 110 yds [100m] per 3½ oz [100g] ball) **5** bulky

Nashua Handknits *Julia* (worsted weight: 50% wool, 25% alpaca, 25% mohair; 93 yds [85m] per 1¾ oz [50g] ball) **3** light

Plymouth *Galway Worsted* or *Highland Heather* (worsted weight; 100% wool; 210 yds [192m] per 3½ oz [100g] ball) **3** light

Red Barn Yarn *Worsted Weight* (worsted weight; 85% wool, 15% mohair; 190 yds [174m] per 4 oz [113.5g] skein): dark chocolate brown (Nora # 7) **4** medium

Shibui *Highland Wool Alpaca* (bulky; 80% wool, 20% alpaca; 255 yds [233m] per 8.8 oz [250g] skein) **5** bulky

Shibui *Silk Cloud* (lace weight; 60% kid mohair, 40% silk; 330 yds [300m] per .88 oz [25g] skein) **0** lace

Stonehedge Fiber Mill *Shepherd's Wool* (fingering weight; 100% merino wool; 230 yds [210m] per 1⅜ oz [39g] skein) **1** super fine

Stonehedge Fiber Mill *Shepherd's Wool* (worsted weight; 100% merino wool; 250 yds [229m] per 4 oz [113.5g] skein) **3** light

Tilli Tomas *Beaded Plié* (double-knitting weight; 100% plied silk with glass beads; 120 yds [110m] per 1½ oz [42.5g] skein) **3** light

Tilli Tomas *Flurries* (worsted weight; 100% merino with glass beads; 77 yds [70m] per 2 oz [57g] skein) **3** light

Tilli Tomas *Plié* (double-knitting weight; 100% plied silk; 125 yds [114m] per 1½ oz [42.5g] skein) **3** light

Universal Yarn *Deluxe Worsted* (worsted weight; 100% wool; 220 yds [201m] per 4 oz [113.5g] skein) **4** medium

Resources

YARN SOURCES

Alpaca with a Twist
950 S. White River Parkway West
Drive
Indianapolis, IN 46221
866-37TWIST
info@alpacawithatwist.com

ArtYarns
39 Westmoreland Avenue
White Plains, NY 10606
914-428-0333
www.artyarns.com

Clover Needlecraft, Inc.
1441 S. Carlos Avenue
Ontario, CA 91761
800-233-1703
customercare@clover-usa.com
www.clover-usa.com

Crystal Palace Yarns
Straw into Gold, Inc.
160 23rd Street
Richmond, CA 94804
cpyinfo@straw.com
www.straw.com

Jade Sapphire
www.jadesapphire.com

Nashua Handknits
165 Ledge Street
Nashua, NH 03060
www.nashuahandknits.com

Plymouth Yarn Company, Inc.
500 Lafayette Street
Bristol, PA 19007
215-788-0459
www.plymouthyarn.com

Red Barn Yarn
450 Rosemont Avenue
Pasadena, CA 91103
626-221-8817
info@redbarnyarn.com
www.redbarnyarn.com

Shibui Knits, LLC
1101 SW Alder Street
Portland, OR 97205
503-595-5898
info@shibuiknits.com
www.shibuiknits.com

Stonehedge Fiber Mill
2246 Pesek Road
East Jordan, MI 49727
231-536-2779
www.stonehedgefibermill.com

Tilli Tomas
617-524-3330
Info@tillitomas.com
www.tillitomas.com

Sunflower Fibers & Tri-Looms by Jim
123 Anderson Street
Fayatteville, NC 28301
937-361-7942
info@sunflowerfibers.com
www.sunflowerfibers.com

Universal Yarn
284 Ann Street
Concord, NC 28025
877-864-9276
sales@universalyarn.com
www.universalyarn.com

Westminster Fibers, Inc.
165 Ledge Street
Nashua, NH 03060
800-445-9276
www.westminsterfibers.com

HARDWARE, MATERIALS & FINDINGS SOURCES

Clover Needlecraft, Inc.
(bamboo double-pointed needles, locking stitch markers, darning and tapestry needles)
1441 S. Carlos Avenue
Ontario, CA 91761
800-233-1703
customercare@clover-usa.com
www.clover-usa.com

Creative Impressions in Clay
(handmade, custom-color, pearl-size, and other fabulous ceramic clay buttons)
6162 Lindsey Court
Liberty Turnpike, OH 45044
513-755-2155
tari@claybuttons.com
www.claybuttons.com

Halcyon Yarn Company
(glass washboards for felting)
12 School Street
Bath, ME 04530
800-341-0282
www.halcyonyarn.com

Hiya Hiya-USA
(stainless-steel hollow double-pointed needles starting at sizes 0–6, and interchangeable stainless-steel circular needles)

The Knitting Zone, Inc.
487 Cabbage Patch Road
Laceys Spring, AL 35754
256-882-2300
sales@hiyahiya-usa.com
www.hiyahiyanorthamerica.com

Noni® Designs, Ltd.
(Noni bag and flower patterns; purse frames, hardware, and custom zippers)
8600 Foundry Street
Carding Studio 108-109
Savage, MD 20763
nora@nonipatterns.com
www.nonipatterns.com

Online Fabric Store
(down-filled pillow forms)
877-805-1023
info@onlinefabricstore.net
www.onlinefabricstore.net

Skacel Collection, Inc.
(Addi-turbo knitting needles)
PO Box 88110
Seattle, WA 98138-2110
800-255-1278
info@skacelknitting.com
www.skacelknitting.com

Sunflower Fibers & Tri-Looms by Jim
(big knitting needles and special-order big double-pointed needle sets)
123 Anderson Street
Fayetteville, NC 28301
910-223-1314
info@sunflowerfibers.com
www.sunflowerfibers.com

The BagSmith
(big knitting needles, big double-pointed needles by special order, and big sewing needles)
20600 Chagrin Boulevard, Suite 101
Shaker Heights, OH 44122
216-921-3500
www.bagsmith.com

Acknowledgments

These acknowledgments are neither wide nor deep enough to encompass all that should be said. The seeds of the book were planted when my mother, Jean Larson, taught me to knit continental style (she was taught by her aunt, Alma Tiolinda, from Sweden) and when she taught me to recognize and name the wildflowers, and when my grandmother took me on tours of her garden, when my father, William Bellows, began weaving rugs and shared a love of handmade things and the natural world with me. Those seeds were nurtured when Margie Kovens asked me to make a felted bag for her, when Pat Rohmer implored me to write my patterns down. My thanks to those who have bought a Noni pattern: Your support has meant that I could devote myself to creating more designs and the flowers for this book.

My editor at Potter Craft, Betty Wong, gave me a great deal of freedom to determine the shape of this project and helped bring it into being in so many ways, first by sending me a note that asked, "I am wondering whether you have any interest in the possibility of doing . . . a book?"

Thanks to the companies that offered yarn for the samples: Alpaca with a Twist, ArtYarns, Crystal Palace, Jade Sapphire, Nashua Handknits/Westminster Fibers, Plymouth Yarn, Red Barn Yarn, Shibui, Stonehedge Fiber Mill, Tilli Tomas, and Universal Yarn. And to those who offered product support: Clover-USA provided bamboo velvet double-points, locking stitch markers, and darning and tapestry needles; Tari Sasser of Creative Impressions in Clay made custom buttons for the May Violets Fingerless Gloves; Halcyon Yarn Company sent a beautiful glass washboard; Hiya Hiya-USA sent its signature stainless-steel double-pointed knitting needles, which I love; Tri-Looms by Jim made me two sets of great big double-points; The BagSmith sent big knitting needles, double-points, and a huge sewing needle to weave in giant ends.

My gratitude to the sunflower and I-cord knitters: Marianne Beasley, Eileen Colligan, Martha DeHaven, Toni Dula, Virginia Finegan, Gina Ganse, Jackie Groff, Rebecca Harris Burns, Jane Hartin, Joan Hauser, Cindy Hays, Regina Hill, Windy Karpavage (who also knit other flower samples), David Keefer, Monicque Larocque, Judy Laszcz, Marcia Melbert, Brenda Miller, Gaile Morrison, Kim Oakey, Demi Porter, Christine Storch, Beth Szabo, Barbara Tanner, Susan Troop, and Ardith Trumpy. Jenifer Johnston made the very first sunflowers and all of those that appear in the sunflower pattern. She would have made many more flowers but for her little girl being born in the middle of all that flower knitting!

Thanks to my dear friend Mary Elliott, who has worked on many Noni projects. Mary made countless flowers, the Forget-Me-Not Pillow (and many more pillows that didn't make it into the photographs but are cherished by me), checked and rechecked the flower patterns with a tirelessness I will never forget.

A special thank-you to Monica Beard, whose knitting is fast and flawless and whose questions always make the work better.

Nancy Yaneth Garcia Navarro is the beautiful model for the projects. Jody Rusnak was more than a fabulous makeup artist and hair stylist.

Thank you to Charlotte Quiggle, whose consistency and tough questions have made their mark on every pattern as she tech-edited the book, offering insight and thoughtful comments.

I am lucky to have Mamochka and Papchik as parents-in-law who love me like their own daughter. They generously gave me the use of their car and cottage on Lake Huron for much longer than they anticipated so that I could have a clean, well-lit place to write (with a well-stocked fridge full of Momachka's cooking!).

Sharon Rutz and her family welcomed me at their Thanksgiving table when I was alone working—I can't adequately express how much that meant to me.

My mother, Jean Larson, used her connections at the National Agricultural Library and her considerable knowledge of the natural world to compile interesting facts for me about each flower. My sister, Laura Bellows, offered nudges when I was stuck, packed orders for Noni when I was away, delighted in the flowers I made, and offered much-needed support.

Sully (R.A. Sullivan Photography), I can't thank you enough for the beautiful photographs in this book, for working with me as one artist with another. I will always be grateful that you shared my vision and adopted a passion for these flowers that brings them to life in these pages.

Kellie Nuss took four beautiful still-life pictures that show how you can live with these flowers. She also made the stephanotis, which awed me with the power of gauge more than I thought it would. She made many samples, asked good questions, and was a steady, invaluable presence as we worked together in my studio.

My deepest gratitude to my husband, Michael, for sending me away to work, and again to him and my little boy, Soma, for sacrificing my presence for the better part of November, the first part of December 2010, and many evenings and weekends in the months that followed. Misha, your engineer's mind, exacting artistic eye and ear, and steadfast support have left their indelible mark on every page of this book.

Flower Index

pg 36
Angel's Tears Daffodil,
Narcissus triandrus

pg 39
Black-Eyed Susan,
Rudbeckia hirta

pg 41
Bloodroot,
Sanguinaria canadensis

pg 43
Cherry Blossom,
Prunus serrulata

pg 45
Chicory,
Cichorium intybus

pg 47
Chionodoxa,
Chionodoxa forbesii
'GLORY OF THE SNOW'

pg 50
Clematis,
Clematis niobe

pg 52
Creeping Phlox,
Phlox subulata

pg 54
Crocus,
Crocus chrysanthus

pg 57
Cyclamen,
Cyclamen hederifolium

pg 59
Daffodil, *Narcissus*
psuedo-narcissus

pg 62
Dahlia,
Dahlia

pg 64
Dogwood,
Cornus florida

pg 66
English Bluebell, *Hyacin-*
thoides non-scripta

pg 68
Forget-Me-Not,
Brunnera macrophylia

pg 69
Fuchsia,
Fuchsia aintree

pg 72
Gardenia,
Gardenia grandiflora

pg 75
Giant White Calla Lily,
Zantedeschia aethiopica

pg 78
Hollyhock,
Alcea rosea

pg 81
Japanese Anemone,
Anemone hybrida

pg 84
Jasmine,
Jasminum officinale

pg 86
Lesser Celandine,
Ranunculus ficaria

pg 88
Madagascar Jasmine,
Stephanotis floribunda

pg 90
Meadowfoam,
Limnanthes douglasii

pg 92
Orange Blossom,
Citrus sinensis

pg 95
Oriental Lily,
Lilium oriental
'CASABLANCA'

pg 99
Pansy,
Viola tricolor

pg 102
Pawpaw Blossom,
Asimina triloba

pg 105
Periwinkle,
Vinca major

pg 107
Pheasant's Eye Daffodil,
Narcissus poeticus

pg 110
Pom-Pom Chrysanthe-
mum, *Dendranthema
morifolium*

pg 112
Purple Shamrock,
Oxalis triangularis

pg 114
Rose,
Rosa multiflora

pg 117
Shirley Poppy,
Papaver rhoeas

pg 120
Star Magnolia,
Magnolia stellata

pg 124
Sunflower,
Helianthus annuus

pg 127
Sweetheart Rose,
Rosa polyantha

pg 129
Tulip,
Tulipa hybrida

pg 132
Wood Violet,
Viola papilionacea

pg 135
Ylang-Ylang,
Cananga odorata

Index